Brilliant ideas

Adventure sports

52 brilliant ideas for taking yourself
to the limit

Steve Shipside

brilliantideas

Careful now...

I can't really believe I have to say this but, just as airline stewards are forced to point out the exits to an audience of people with their noses in their magazines, no book on adventure sports is complete without a warning. So here it goes. Oddly we can't breathe water, so plunging into it comes with an inherent risk. Throwing yourself off bridges, jumping out of aeroplanes, rushing down hills with no brakes, even going for a walk in the wilderness all have associated dangers and yes, you can die. For pretty much all of the sports here the first step is to sign a little waiver saying that if you die it's your fault. This book comes with exactly the same advice.

So use your head. Don't get drawn into someone else's idea of acceptable risk if you don't feel safe. Don't trust your life to cowboys or hooligans high on adrenaline. Do get medical advice before taking yourself to limits you've never before tried. And, above all, if you end up bent, broken or roadkill don't come running to me or the publishers because as much as we love you we don't have a penny to make it all better and we formally renounce all responsibility. It's your life, now go out and make sure it lives up to that description.

Although the contents of this book were checked at the time of going to press, the world keeps moving and the World Wide Web does so twice as fast. This means the publisher and author cannot guarantee the contents of any of the websites mentioned in the text.

First published in 2006 by
The Infinite Ideas Company Limited
36 St Giles
Oxford
OX1 3LD
United Kingdom
www.infideas.com

CIP catalogue records for this book are available from the British Library and the US Library of Congress.

ISBN 1-904902-52-9

Brand and product names are trademarks or registered trademarks of their respective owners.

Designed and typeset by Baseline Arts Ltd, Oxford
Printed and bound by TJ International, Cornwall

Brilliant features

Each chapter of this book is designed to provide you with an inspirational idea that you can read quickly and put into practice straight away.

Throughout you'll find four features that will help you to get right to the heart of the idea:

■ *Try another idea* If this idea looks like a life-changer then there's no time to lose. *Try another idea* will point you straight to a related tip to expand and enhance the first.

■ *Here's an idea for you* Give it a go – right here, right now – and get an idea of how well you're doing so far.

■ *Defining ideas* Words of wisdom from masters and mistresses of the art, plus some interesting hangers-on.

■ *How did it go?* If at first you do succeed try to hide your amazement. If, on the other hand, you don't this is where you'll find a Q and A that highlights common problems and how to get over them.

Introduction

One person's adventure sport is another's walk in the park. There is no real definition of what is or is not an 'adventure' sport simply because we all have a different notion of what adventure is. Which is precisely what is so wonderful about the sports in this book.

Personally, I think an adventure sport is pretty much anything where taking part involves setting yourself an element of challenge. How far down that route you want to go is up to you. Each individual should set her own bar when it comes to risk, and draw her own line in the sand at the point where peeking over it gives a delicious thrill of danger. That could be BASE jumping off the Eiffel Tower, it could be a hike up an unknown hill. Don't let anyone else try to tell you what is your idea of adventure, just enjoy it as it is.

Because of that element of individual boundaries, adventure sports are not usually team affairs (although there are exceptions such as adventure racing or cave diving), rather a very personal exploration of limits. They tend to be less organised and have few formal rules (other than having fun and staying alive). That alone is enough to appeal to whole groups of people who would never have seen themselves as sporty. At one time the outer edge of holiday sport was donkey rides on the beach. Now you're more likely to be offered scuba diving, SCAD diving and surfing – the choice is endless and the rewards can be surprising. Whether it's the teenager who is turned off by team sports at school or the grandma rebelling against being forced into a life of crown green bowls and coffee mornings, adventure sports offer a different approach for everyone. Which is one of the reasons I've avoided the term 'extreme' sport. Many adventure sports are extreme sports – anyone who throws themselves off buildings or races down hills lying flat on an elongated skateboard can call themselves extreme with little risk of quibbling. The term itself, though, has connotations of an exclusive set of young, 'rad' dudes with tribal tattoos and some fabulously imaginative piercings. Nothing wrong with that, just that the whole joy of adventure sport should be its inclusiveness. Adventure sports are all about having a go, not about being excluded because some smart marketing people have hijacked an activity, packaged it and sold it to a 'target market'. So don't worry about what people will think, just get out there and have a go – and then another go.

Adventure sports thrive by nicking ideas from each other – skateboarding copied surfing, snowboarding copied skateboarding, sand boarding copied snowboarding and so the skills and thrills of one can, and should, be applied to others. You may find that you turn out to be good at something you never dreamt you could do. Or you could be hopeless but have the time of your life doing it. Either way the following should be seen not as some kind of defining list but as a menu of potential pleasures, a smorgasbord of sports you may not have heard of, let alone tried.

There's a saying amongst adventure sports people that 'if you're not living on the edge you're taking up too much space'. It's up to you to decide where that edge is, but when you've done so you should creep up to it and sneak a peek over the side. Whatever you do, don't forget to enjoy the ride while you're at it.

1

Twenty inches of pure joy

There are two types of people in this world. The ones who can't say 'BMX' without getting a gleam in their eyes, and the ones who say 'why are your wheels so small?'.

BMX means Bicycle Motocross; it emerged from the US in the 70s as kids emulated motocross riders with their frantic races over bumps and ramps, often finding themselves flung in the air as they went.

There are different species of BMX bikes, but the identifying characteristics for all breeds include twenty-inch wheels, only one gear and much smaller forks than mountain bikes. They're quite distinct; here's a summary.

Dirt bikes are solid-looking critters with no front brake. Dirt bikes are used for riding races on lanes over soil ramps, often combined as double ramps (take-off on the first, land on the second) and jumps are often combined with crowd-pleasing aerial stunts.

Here's an idea for you...

The bunny-hop is one of those building-block tricks you need to get the hang of before you can build up to other, more complex moves. It means jumping without a ramp and is the commonest way of getting up onto kerbs, etc., with style. Bend your knees, lean back and yank the front wheel up; when it's off the ground use your legs to lift up the back wheel. When you can consistently hop and hop high then try lining yourself up alongside objects (say a log) and from a stationary start bunny-hopping sideways right over them.

Race bikes were the original BMX bikes. Quite simply, they're a human-powered version of the motorised motocross. Race bikes are cut back to the absolute basics and designed for flat-out racing on a dirt track with jumps (stunts are usually abandoned in racing though it wouldn't be BMX if there wasn't the occasional show-off). Frame pads may be fitted to protect the rider and helmets and gloves are definitely a good idea.

Street/ramp bikes have pegs to grind and smooth-surfaced tyres. Street riding is about tricks, jumping off stairs and grinding on rails, basically all the stuff you see skateboarders doing but with two wheels instead of four. Ramp riding is about tricks performed in half pipes or larger vert ramps (which have a purely vertical sheer to them just below the coping). You've probably seen BMXers pulling tricks on MTV et al. in vert ramps as they shoot up to the coping, pull tricks, turn and land back in the ramp.

Flatland bikes have straight spokes with brakes front and back and are typically lightweight to help with flinging them around

For more urban wheelie fun take a look at IDEA 50, *Sk8.*

Try another idea...

for tricks. Flatlanders are all-round bikes and flatland tricks don't involve ramps or street furniture but a simple flat space (hence the name) and an amazingly good sense of balance. Flatland tricks usually involve balancing on one wheel or performing gymnastics while twirling the bike beneath you. Take the backwards steamroller, for example – spin the handlebars right round. Stand at the front of the bike facing the seat and holding it in one hand. One foot rests on a front peg (which projects from the hub) while the other pushes off. Steer with the handlebars, lift the back wheel off the ground by the seat and roll the bike backwards, balancing vertically.

There are two quite distinct generations of those for whom the words 'BMX' bring a sparkle to the eyes. The original generation, for whom BMXs emerged at around the same time as skateboards, and a more modern group altogether who have taken to flatland style and ramp biking largely thanks to their presence at the X and Gravity Games. Despite the age difference both groups seem to coexist quite amicably wherever they come together.

'When I was a kid I used to pray every night for a new bicycle. Then I realised that the Lord doesn't work that way so I stole one and asked Him to forgive me.'
EMO PHILIPS, comedian

Defining idea...

How did
it go?

Q **I'm told I have to be able to do an endo to get anywhere with flatland tricks, so what's an endo?**

A *It's more of a starting move than a trick in its own right and one that's well worth mastering if you want to go further. Start off by rolling forward, standing on the pedals. Lean forwards and slam on the front brake so your back tyre comes off the ground (also known in some circles as a 'stoppie'). Keep the back wheel as high off the ground as you can without going over the handlebars (a tad uncool), balance for as long as you can, then drop the back tyre and cycle off looking like you do that all the time.*

Q **Why would I want to learn the backwards steamroller?**

A *Simply because it's a great introduction to one-wheel balancing tricks and one of the few that don't involve scuffing the wheel or feathering the brakes so all you're really focusing on (for the moment at least) is the balance.*

Q **Can I try these tricks with my mountain bike?**

A *Try, yes, succeed – not sure. The flatlander bikes have a number of design features aimed purely at stunts, including the ability to turn the handlebars right round without fouling the brake cables, and smooth tyres, rather than knobblies. Plus their dinky frames and wheels give them a low centre of gravity. You can certainly pull an endo with a mountain bike, but without pegs you're going to remain a spectator when it comes to something like a backwards steamroller.*

2

Heroes of Telemark

Imagine downhill skis that can also handle rough terrain, uphill and touring. Telemark skiing manages all of those – provided you've got thighs like Arnie, naturally.

Telemark is a type of free-heel skiing (one where the heel isn't attached to the ski) in which the back leg is bent at the knee, bringing the skier much closer to the snow.

If you're having trouble picturing that then think of Olympic ski jumpers as they prepare to land with one foot forwards and the other bent behind them (they also use free-heels). Personally, I don't have any trouble picturing Telemark skiing because I first encountered it years ago when a Norwegian friend came swishing towards me on positively anorexic skis and holding what looked like a quarterstaff instead of poles. Given that he was down on one knee I could only presume that he had either mistaken me for royalty/the pope, or was intending to propose marriage.

 When I pointed this out to him he had a bit of a Scandiwegian hissy fit and told me he was practicing a fine Norwegian ski technique that positively oozed class. I couldn't help but feel he would have oozed a little more class if he hadn't been wearing what seemed to be hob-nailed boots and knee socks but since then, as now,

The other point that may seem tricky for Alpine skiers to get to grips with is the way that the pointing of the skis comes not from the hips but from the feet. Try this little drill to get the idea. Simply raise each foot in turn and get used to twisting and turning it so that your ski moves around parallel to the ground. The trick is to concentrate on ensuring that the movement comes from the knee downwards – everything above the knee should remain rock solid. Get that and you're half way to understanding the Telemark approach to steering, not to mention working on the balance essential to the technique.

I found it a full time job just to stay upright on skis it seemed better to let the point pass. Watching him in horrified fascination as he genuflected his way around the slopes I started to notice that he seemed to be breaking all the rules, or the rules as they were understood by a soggy-arsed Brit novice anyway. For a start he went on or off-piste as he chose. Secondly he scorned ski lifts in favour of putting 'skins' on his lightweight skis and stomping off uphill on them. Best of all, when the day was done he slipped his skis off and walked to the bar in the leather boots, without slipping once. If it wasn't for the knee socks he might have looked quite classy at that point. Had I but known it, his curious bent-knee stance also meant he was also well down the path towards building the kind of thigh muscles Nureyev would have been proud of.

Telemark is similar to cross-country skiing in that both have the free heel, but the true Telemark gear is rather different since Telemark skis have stiff ankle support, edges and bindings that either hold the boot to the ski at the toe only or that use a cable to clip around the boot (although quick releases are now appearing). The big advantage is that the overall result is a very light ski which only needs 'skins' to be attached to the ski for grip and you can walk up hill or get right off the piste – making Telemark well suited to touring mountains.

Telemark skiers tend to be fiercely proud of resurrecting this traditional technique, and dedicated to proving just how liberating it can be. Such is their dedication that at least one practitioner has combined paragliding and Telemark to come up with para-Telemark; possibly the ultimate mountain exploration technique.

If you're looking for more snow-related fun, try snowboarding: skim through IDEA 9, *Surfing on snow*.

Try another idea...

Free-heel skis require a distinctive technique for downhill turns called, predictably, the Telemark turn. This involves sliding the outer (downhill) ski ahead of the other as it moves in the direction of the turn while bending the knee on the inner ski and lifting the heel.

Sounds confusing? Try practising by standing with your weight equally distributed on both feet and sliding your left foot back at the same time as you slide your right foot forward. When you're used to the feel of both feet sliding in opposite directions try to get into the habit of bending your knees at the end of the slide, and rising up taller as they pass each other. That's the basic move of the transition from one foot to the other into a turn. Now try hopping as you make the transition so that both feet leave the ground. You'll know you've got it when you find that you land perfectly balanced with the weight equally distributed on both feet and the back heel lifted off the ski.

'If you are going to try cross-country skiing, start with a small country.'
Traditional advice to the Telemarker

Defining idea...

How did it go?

Q   Can I Telemark on a snowboard, then?

A   *Hmm. You're having a laugh, aren't you? Well, funnily enough, while you can't Telemark as such, there is still a way of heading for the back country and snowboarding without ski lifts. There is such a thing as a split board – a board that splits into two 'skis' which can be skinned to climb with, then bound back together again to make a single board.*

Q   I really want to ski tour but do I have to learn true Telemark technique to do it?

A   *No. If you're interested in the idea of being able to tour, but don't want to learn Telemark technique then there are also AT (Alpine Touring) free-heel bindings where you can release the heel to walk uphill, then fix it again. It's also possible to use a touring adapter plate, which you insert into the bindings to allow uphill climbs with a free heel, before removing it for downhilling. Just don't tell the purists.*

3

Solid sky – ice diving

Slipping into icy water where your breath bubbles up against a gleaming ice ceiling is all part of the appeal in the eerily beautiful, chillingly dangerous world of ice diving.

Why do people ice dive? Well it probably started amongst those for whom half the year means ice diving or nothing.

Divers in the far north are used to seeing their favourite lakes (and in some cases seas) turn solid for months of the year and a combination of frustration, curiosity and boredom probably led to the earlier ice divers breaking out the saws and seeing what was going on underneath. What they found was to inspire a whole new sport.

When the ice takes over the surface it has a number of effects on water. It shields it from wind and thus waves too, and so makes it calmer. It can act as an insulator resulting in steady (if none too warm) temperatures and yet it restricts the amount of sunlight and this, combined with the cold, results in less algal growth in the water. The overall result is massively improved underwater visibility. Of course, you might wonder what there is to see in a frozen lake, but the answer is that life goes on much as usual, if a little slower, with the bonus that the ice itself is now there to wonder at – a gleaming icing crust laid over the top of a crystal-clear aquarium.

Here's an idea for you...

Before you ice dive you should train as an ice diver – logical enough, really, and as well as local courses run by specialist clubs you will also find that the big dive organisations such as PADI (Professional Association of Dive Instructors) have an ice-diving course on their books. Typically a course will require you to be eighteen or more and already qualified as an open water diver. They run for about twelve hours and include three dives over two days during which you will cover planning, organisation, techniques, safety and potential glitches. It's well worth the time and counts as a specialty cert towards your Master Scuba Diver rating (touted as the 'black belt' of diving).

Inspired by what they found under iced-over lakes divers have looked further afield for chilly challenges and that has led them to the Arctic where deep ice covers large stretches of diveable sea. Where there is semi-permanent sea ice there are also astonishing formations of ice stalactites, ice walls, ice caves and entire blue-white cathedrals of solid water to be discovered and dived. Ice divers will rave about the breathtaking beauty of the effect of sunlight filtered through ice formations. As soon as their teeth stop chattering, that is.

Ice diving is also pretty much the only way you are ever going to get to see certain types of wildlife. Number one on the ice diver's tick list of creatures to chase after is undoubtedly the Greenland shark, a huge (the fourth largest shark in the world), slow-swimming, sleepy-eyed beast that cruises just beneath the ice searching for carrion. Whales and seals are also occasional swimming partners, not least since, like divers, they are on the lookout for air holes in the ice.

Ice is what's classed as an 'overhead environment' which claustrophobes will have picked up on straight away. It's considered potentially dangerous to dive just because you don't have the option of bolting for the surface if anything goes wrong. Well, you do, but it won't do you a lot of good because someone put a cold ceiling in the way. Diving in overhead environments, whether they be ice, caverns or wrecks, involves particular care in planning and safety.

Serious about diving in overhead environments? Like testing yourself to the technical extreme? Then the ultimate is undoubtedly diving underground – see IDEA 8, *Cave diving*.

Try another idea...

In order to ice dive, a hole must first be cut in the ice and in order to ice dive safely it must be possible for a diver to find that hole whatever happens. Which is where the special procedures of ice diving come into play. Ice diving is conducted within the 'light zone' and usually within immediate sight of the entry hole (which is carved out with augers and chainsaws). In addition, safety lines and harnesses physically attach the diver to an ice screw drilled into the ice at the surface. In an emergency the lines are strong enough for the surface crew to haul a diver back. Dry suits are a must and regulators must be of the environmentally-sealed variety to avoid icing up.

'Cold! If the thermometer had been an inch longer we'd have frozen to death.'
MARK TWAIN

Defining idea...

How did it go?

Q **I have a double 7 mm semi-dry suit which has served me well in places such as Scapa Flow in the Orkneys – will I be OK in that?**

A *Frankly, no. If ever there was a case for dry suits then ice diving is it. If you don't have your own then beg, borrow or steal one. Or you could ask to rent one from the ice divers you are going with. (You're not going on your own, are you?!)*

Q **I dived ice. I loved it, but I froze my feet off and stopped thinking about anything other than the cold after ten minutes. I'm already wearing a dry suit and all the clothes I own underneath, what else can I do?**

A *You can ask about the use of argon gas to fill your suit. Argon is a spectacularly good insulator and tech divers in seriously cold environments hook up an argon cylinder to their dry suit instead of filling it from the air tanks.*

4

A leg at each corner – horse trekking

Trekking through foreign lands is a fabulous way to get close up to the wilderness but why not let someone else do all the legwork?

Especially if that someone happens to have <u>two</u> pairs of legs at their disposal.

Having had a go at falling off almost anything with a board or wheels it was inevitable that someone would one day suggest I tried my hand at tumbling off big hairy things with a surplus of legs. As a hardened city slicker I have always been wary of horsey people, so it came as a pleasant surprise to find that the world of horse trekking is, by and large, amazingly easy and laid-back. If there is a pitfall, it is that it can be just a little bit too laid-back. If you're planning on a dedicated trekking trip with a professional outfit then you have little to worry about – that's their job. If, as is so often the case however, your trekking is likely to be a largely impromptu decision based on a local operator's suggestion, then there are a few questions you may want to ask:

What kind of tuition will there be? This is a quick way to tell cowboys from cowboy operators. Everyone will say they offer tuition, but for some that means showing you which end is the front before leaving you to your own devices. Even if

Try combining horse trekking and water. There is nothing more satisfying than riding on a beach and urging the horse into the water. Or crossing rivers. Apart from an oddly at-one-with-nature feeling about riding above the waters on a large animal it is a great way to see wildlife. In Venezuela, for example, pony trekking is one of the best ways to get up close and personal with the capybara and anaconda.

you are already a confident rider, you can get the measure of the operator by listening to what they think is sufficient tuition for the route they are planning to take you on.

Can you take a look at the horses in advance? In developing countries anyone with a horse suddenly becomes a trekking operator, but when you get to look at the animals you may find they're in poor condition. Such animals will probably only start to look lively as they approach home and hay at the end of your trek. There are other considerations. I once went pony trekking in Iceland where they have a unique breed of beast descended from Viking mounts. They were gorgeous and knew their way around the tundra like pros. Unfortunately they were also knee-high to a vole, every single one of them, which would have ruled them out for tall people.

What kind of saddles do they have? The American-style saddle with a high pommel is great for beginners as you can just sit in it like an armchair and cling to the pommel when it gets bumpy. European style is less comfy, more slimline and unforgiving. Saddles made of carpet and reins made of old rope are best avoided altogether.

If you've chosen the right trek tour you'll get all the advice you need from them. Just in case you're not sure however, here are some tips for getting on with your big new hairy friend.

- Leading the horse is best done by walking level with its head and turning it by leading it around the outside of you – don't try turning by walking across its front or you'll end up pushing against half a ton of horse while trying to avoid the hooves.

For those who trust Shanks's pony rather than the four-legged variety, there is always traditional trekking – see **IDEA 27, *Trekking*,** for more.

Try another idea...

- Going through a gate means leading the horse all the way through, probably turning it around so that you are able to shut the gate again. Don't expect the horse to make room for your legs as you go through together.

- As you mount the horse make sure you have the reins in your hand but not held so tightly that you pull the horse's head back as you swing onto the saddle. Failing to hold the reins means that your horse is very likely to wander off just as you are trying to get up – cue hilarity all round.

- Keep the reins in your hands, which should be centred in front and low. Don't have too much slack otherwise when it comes time to rein in you'll have to pull right back which will shift your own weight backwards and destabilise you.

- Nudging the horse (you shouldn't have to kick it) takes it up a gear and doing it again takes it up another gear, though for much trekking a walk is the fastest speed you will have to worry about.

- If you do want to break into a trot then rise and fall with the motion of the horse. To help that, keep your heels down, close into the sides of the horse. While the weight is

'*A horse is dangerous at both ends and uncomfortable in the middle.*'
IAN FLEMING

Defining idea...

15

distributed down the whole of your leg the impetus comes from the heels
(which is why they are kept firmly down).

■ If the horse wants to pee you should stand up in the saddle – something to do
with kidney pressure, it seems.

Q **I find trotting amazingly hard – am I destined to proceed forever
at a walking pace?**

A *Have you tried cantering? Nudge the beastie up a gear from the trot and
you'll find that while it is faster it is also a much smoother movement, and
so is more comfortable and easier to master.*

Q **The damn thing has a mind of its own – it stops and eats when it
wants to and won't do what I tell it. What do I do?**

A *You could try changing horses but it's likely you're not showing it who's in
control. Be firm but very clear with your movements. If you're moving your
hands and arms around a lot (shifting the reins from hand to hand, for
example) you may be sending confusing messages. It may have a mind of
its own, but Einstein it ain't.*

5
Lighter than air

Ballooning is more like a state of mind than a means of getting airborne.

While other forms of flight involve constant adjustment of controls, balloonists simply soar aloft and drift silently to whatever destination nature chooses for them.

You don't steer a balloon. That doesn't mean you have no control over where you're going – advanced knowledge of the likely winds and the ability to read air patterns means a balloon pilot can place their craft pretty accurately in the path of winds going the way they want. Other than rising or falling, however, that's the limit of the control. For some that sounds like a limitation. For others it is the ultimate liberation and the reason why ballooning makes more sense now than at any time in its long history.

Tethered balloons sometimes pop up at fairs and air shows, allowing the opportunity to grab a quick ride into the sky to gawp at the view, or to leap out and trust your life to a parachute or bungee rope. For most of us, however, the first real trip is likely to be a half-day flight over the countryside. The bad news is that there are no lie-ins for balloonists and your trip is likely to start early in the morning.

Here's an idea for you... **Want to learn about getting airborne without paying for it? Every balloon launch requires a couple of crew to help rig up the craft, hold the balloon while it is being filled with hot air, then follow it on the ground and help pack it up again. It's spear-carrying stuff and very few flight schools pay their crew but on the other hand they usually will thank you with balloon rides or flying lessons. If you have a little free time then crewing is the ideal way to find out if ballooning is for you.**

That's because the wind is at its calmest with the sun low in the sky. As the sun gets higher its effects are stronger (think about the danger hours for sunburn) and that means it heats up areas of the ground more. Hot patches of ground heat the air above them, which becomes less dense and rises causing cold air to rush in to fill the gap; there you get breezes and winds. Good news for gliders, bad news for balloons.

Arriving at the balloon launch site you will probably find the balloon itself laid out like a huge squid with the basket at one end and the envelope (the balloon bit) being stretched out prior to filling. With a good ground crew it only takes fifteen to twenty minutes to launch a balloon, including the time it takes to fill the envelope with hot air, usually done by burning propane gas from cylinders in the basket. After that the balloon rises and, apart from the occasional whooshing noise of the propane burners when the pilot wants to rise higher, the rest of the ride is in spectacular silence. If you look below you there will be a chase car somewhere on the ground which is following you. When the balloon lands after a hard day's bobbing around it will be packed back into the car, which also provides transport back to where you started.

Because of the effect of having the sun high in the sky balloons usually land and remain grounded around the middle of day so while ballooning is bad for your breakfast, it does lend itself to some seriously splendid lunching.

If the idea of simple, silent flight gives you a lift then take a look IDEA 32, Paragliding.

Try another idea...

It is possible for balloons to fly at night, but night flights are sadly rare due to the problems of visibility and the need for pilots to rely on instruments and lights (which most balloons don't carry anyway).

Balloons aren't the only things that go to ground during the heat of midday and that's just one of the reasons why balloon safaris have become hugely popular. Starting in the cool early morning, the balloon lifts off and flies low over the landscape, its round shape, slow movement, and total silence combining to make it unthreatening to animals on the ground. As things heat up the balloon comes to ground. A chase car has usually beaten you to it and there'll be collapsing tables and chairs ready for a major blowout of your own.

'Nobody can be uncheered with a balloon.'
Winnie the Pooh, courtesy of A.A. MILNE

Defining idea...

How did it go?

Q   I was just thinking. I'm going for a whole day's ballooning with a friend and a crate of champagne. How do you go to the loo while you're up there?

A   *The simple answer is you don't, so plan ahead. After a bottle of bubbly, blokes tend to get the sudden urge to balance on the edge of the basket while imitating a signpost. This is considered to be poor form.*

Q   Tried it, loved it, want my own. How realistic is that?

A   *Not as unrealistic as you might think. Many people form syndicates and club together to buy a balloon. You'll need a licence to fly one (a balloon is a registered aircraft, just like any other) and in the UK that means sixteen hours of flight experience (including four flights with an instructor), exams in aviation law, meteorology, navigation and balloons, and a test flight with an examiner. It may sound like a lot but the emphasis is on common sense, rather than rocket science. Find out more about ballooning in the UK at www.bbac.org or in the US at www.launch.net.*

6

Street luge

Imagine hurtling down a hill feet first, just centimetres from the road surface.

Did I mention that you have no brakes? If you're not hiding behind your hands at the thought then maybe street luge is for you.

Street luge may have borrowed its name from the language of bobsledding but its real origins lie far from the glamour and glistening ice of the Cresta run. The simple truth is that a street luge is nothing more than an extended skateboard and it developed from boarders trying to reach faster speeds by lying down on their boards. At that point it went by the very slightly more knockabout name of 'butt boarding', which was never going to get it much media attention, let alone corporate sponsorship. The first pure skateboard speed races started in the mid-70s at Signal Hill in California and the word 'luge' became associated with the prone riding position. The sport really got its time in the sun in the mid-90s when those dashing marketeers at ESPN rolled it into the X Games. Then the whole world could see street lugers in action and ask, as one, 'why?'

It's still a pretty good question. Steering is done by means of skateboard 'trucks' (sprung axles) which means that you can only dictate where you are going by leaning that way. Brakes are actually forbidden in competition (who needs 'em –

Here's an idea for you...

You don't have to commit to the full-on street luge experience to go downhilling in urban areas. There is a halfway house called a skate luge. A skate luge is a hybrid between a skateboard and a toboggan. You sit on it like a toboggan, and it has handy rails down the side to hang on to, but it rides on skateboard trucks and is steered by shifting your weight from one side to the other. You're sitting up which feels much safer than lying down and (promise you won't tell anybody this) there is even the option of a hand-operated button which leads to (remember you promised) an actual brake.

they only slow you down anyway, dude) so the only way to stop is with your heavily reinforced boots and gloves. Or by running out of hill. Or, even more spectacularly, by getting over-familiar with a car, since the sport is practised on roads.

By and large it is not illegal per se (except, ironically, in one part of California), though the police have any number of ways of hoiking you off the highway, depending on which part of the world you live in. Apart from anything else you are more than likely to break the speed limit in residential areas – street lugers have been clocked at well over 100 km/h.

Obviously the trick to trying it out is to find a safe place to practise but this is not always easy unless you happen to have a private road to call your own. Don't necessarily expect help from other lugers, by the way, since good strips are often jealously guarded for fear that new riders will have accidents or otherwise draw unwanted attention to a choice location.

As for finding a board, the simple answer is that most people make their own out of metal, wood or, if they have the funds and the know-how, from more space-age materials like carbon fibre. Protection comes in the form of motorbiking gear, usually including full leathers, a full helmet, and boots/gloves. Those that can afford it go the whole hog and invest in large amounts of Kevlar body armour which can often be incorporated into modern motorbike outfits. You should, by now, be getting the idea that the risks involved in wiping out extend far beyond the odd graze or bloody knee.

If you really get into it then you'll be glad to know there are a number of forms of racing, either time trials (individually or in pairs) or mass races on a first past the post basis. These are largely in the US but do pop up as far afield as Austria and Australia – for an idea of the rules take a look at www.gravitysportsinternational.com/rules.html. There are groups that teach street luge in a safe environment but to date these seem to be based solely in the US. If that suits you then check out Gravity Sports' home page.

If street luge is just a way of recapturing your skateboarding youth then who are you kidding – cut straight to the real deal, whatever your age, with IDEA 50, *Sk8*.

Try another idea...

'Luge strategy? Lie flat and try not to die.'
– ANON, but curiously well-informed

Defining idea...

How did it go?

Q   Is there anything I can do to make it safer? In particular to convince my friends/parents/lawyers that I'm not mad?

A   *Yes, obviously entering only events endorsed by one of the major organisers would go a long way but if you're practising then find a genuinely private road, get a marshal or two, set up hay bales as soft crash points and ensure that someone (who is not taking part) is medically trained and has a mobile to call for help if needed.*

Q   If I try a skate luge with a braking system (don't worry, I won't tell anyone) does that mean I can forget about the lumpy protective clothing?

A   *Only if gravel rash is your idea of fun. Even with a brake operating the wheels you'd be well advised to practise braking by dragging your feet, which means boots, and sooner or later you're going to take a tumble so helmet, elbow, knee and hand protectors are a great idea.*

7

A taste for adventure

Once it was the marathon that captured the public imagination, then triathlon took the limelight. Now adventure racing is fast becoming the aspirational adventure sport of the millennium.

Adventure racing is a mutant hybrid between triathlon and full-on exploration expeditions.

There's a lot of terrain between those two points, of course, and there are a lot of different sizes and levels of adventure race springing up to fill the spaces. There are beginner-level events taking an afternoon and leaving the racers exhilarated and a little breathless. At the other extreme are multi-day, end-of-the-earth adventures seemingly put together by disaster film buffs. There are, however, a few points that they all have in common.

While there will always be competitive teams racing each other a lot of the emphasis of adventure racing is to get away from clockwatching and focus more on the experience. When marathoning went from something you read about to something your neighbour did, it also shifted from an event where completing one was an achievement to becoming a cue for comparing personal bests. While every

Here's an idea for you...

There are such things as training courses. Based over one or two days these introduce you to techniques for the commonest elements and then usually put you to the test with a short race combining them. Grab some friends, book in advance to get your place ahead of the corporate groups and have a go. In the UK have a look at Ace Races (www.aceraces.com). Worldwide details can be found in running magazines and on adventure racing websites such as www.sleepmonsters.com and www.worldar.com.

adventure race is against the clock, it is wildly unrealistic to compare times from one to another. Plus, adventure racing is a team event, often specifying at least one man or woman in each team. Which means that a lot more of the skills involved revolve around teamwork, personality and psychology. Adventure races go out of their way to challenge the participants, often including sections that have to be completed on horseback (usually without sufficient horses for the whole team), or Tyrolean traverse (crossing gorges while slung under a giant washing line) or river crossings by inflatable banana.

Many races take that one step further by refusing to tell you what you're going to encounter and making a point of adding surprise challenges en route. Before the event starts you will be told of the major disciplines (rope climbing, mountain biking, trail running, rafting, etc.) then on the day you will usually be given the route and told to make your way together to the next waypoint by the means specified. The only constants are that you are going to be fully exposed to the elements, will almost certainly get covered in mud and are likely to come a lot closer to creepy-crawlies than you'd like. If it's a longer course (several days) then you can add to that the fact that you'll not get enough sleep and you'll lose your sense of humour at some point. How well you cope defines your ability as a racer at least at much as how fast you run or how limitless your endurance might be. You can't leave a team member behind, by the way, no matter how annoying they turn out to be.

Adventure racing is pretty much what the military have been doing in training for years but with more laughs thrown in. It's no longer exclusively a sport for the great outdoors as urban adventure races have now sprung up (check out the Wild Onion at www.urbanadventureracing.com). Urban adventure races tend to throw activities like stair climbing and in-line skating into the mix, but otherwise the principle is much the same. A few of the essential skills you will need are:

- A great sense of humour – that means laughing at yourself, not just the Simpsons.
- A fair level of fitness – think about this relative to the demands of the race and the fitness of your teammates.
- A sense of direction – map reading and orienteering are often key ingredients.
- The ability to ride a bike – even if it was only when you were a kid.
- The ability to swim – preferably while fully dressed and usually when you don't mean to.
- A head for heights – not always needed, but if you're going to go weak at the knees getting over a moderate obstacle then it may be better to stick with bowling.

If you've enjoyed adventure races then perhaps it's time to set your sights on the really big stuff – take a look at IDEA 11, This is a raid!

Try another idea...

'An adventure is only an inconvenience rightly considered. An inconvenience is only an adventure wrongly considered.'
G.K. CHESTERTON

Defining idea...

How did it go?

Q   **I tried it but my teammates turned out to be a bunch of lily-livered, lolling-limbed poltroons. How do I get to sign up with a harder bunch?**

A   *Unless you're right at the top of this game (in which case the other top teams will see your sporting exploits on TV and give you a call) then you'd probably best start with a touch of diplomacy. More experienced teams will be suspicious of anyone who doesn't seem to respect their teammates, however pathetic they may be. Probably the best thing to do is to ask around an existing sports club (triathlon clubs usually yield the best results) to find out if there is another team in the making. You could always try to put together your own. Some websites help put you in touch with other would-be racers; check out those mentioned in 'Here's an idea for you' for starters.*

Q   **I tried and am game for pretty much anything but I just can't run and that dragged the whole team down. Should I give up now?**

A   *No. Look instead for events where either there is no running or a 'ride and run'. In ride and run, the running is part of a leg where a number of bicycles/horses/elephants are shared amongst the team to get to the next checkpoint. The idea is to take turns but if you have a strong runner in your team you may well fare better if you come to an agreement – you hog the bicycle/beastie and they do the extra kilometres on foot.*

8

Cave diving

Descending through crystal-clear water past freakish rock formations in flooded caves is not for everyone. But it may be the closest you can get to the experience of exploring another planet.

Underwater caves are another world, a world seemingly provided with its own geology, atmosphere and physics.

Cave diving, particularly in favourite locations such as Florida and the Dordogne, offers stunning visibility through glass-like water, with no waves, surge or swell. It is like nothing else, and every single dive is guaranteed to be a pulse raiser – there is no such thing as a dull cave dive. Plus, the knowledge, skills and judgement required to cave dive mean that any scuba-diving spelunker can justifiably see themselves as belonging to an elite group.

The other-worldliness of cave diving is undoubtedly one of the biggest thrills of the sport, with the battle to keep a lid on claustrophobia often coming a close second. Seasoned cave divers will always tell you, however, that while they welcome newcomers with a hunger for exploration, they could really do without those in search of an adrenalin high. True cave diving goes well beyond the limits of

Here's an idea for you...

If you're fascinated by the idea of cave diving but (understandably) put off by the risks and technical skills involved, then try cavern diving instead. Cavern diving involves exploring underwater 'overhead environments' but all the while remaining within sight of the entrance (though a guideline is still used for safety reasons). Cavern divers remain within the 40 m of normal recreational diving which means that there are specialty cavern certification courses from the major dive bodies such as NAUI and PADI. Unlike cave divers, cavern divers use standard equipment but will still be expected to learn and develop advanced buoyancy and navigation skills, which will stand them in good stead if they ever choose to go further and try cave diving.

recreational diving and requires technical equipment and extensive training in its use, as well as a sound respect for certain basic rules:

- Get proper training, and stay within the limits of your training. True, there are commercial sites catering for 'ordinary' divers, such as Ginnie Springs or the Blue Grotto in Florida, but elsewhere you must take the appropriate local course and learn about the conditions and how to prepare for them.

- Keep a guideline to the exit. It's easy enough to get disoriented underwater without being in a maze with the floor above your head. Learning navigation is part of the answer but a reel and guidelines complete the picture.

- Carry a light, a backup light and a backup backup light. Of course a backup to the third light isn't a bad idea either.

■ Choose the right breathing mixture and respect its limits. Nitrogen narcosis will kick in if you are breathing air below 30 m and an underwater cave is no place to be ripped to the gills. Stick with the mixtures and limits they teach you about in the local course.

■ The two-thirds rule is time-honoured and still stands: when you are a third of your way through the gas you began with it is time to start your exit. None of this 'surfacing on 50 bar' stuff you learn when bobbing around a few metres from a boat – in cave diving you have to leave two-thirds of your breathing mixture for the task of getting out of there.

■ Listen to the locals; don't go applying cave rules from one location to another. British cave divers snort at the rules of diving from Florida. They will tell you that back-mounted tanks are potentially fatal in the tiny cave entrances in the UK, that helmets are essential and that solo diving is often safer because there is nobody to block your exit in a crisis. If you are cave diving in Britain the advice of the Cave Diving Group overrides anything you may have been taught in France or Florida. Seek it out.

Try another idea...

If you're looking to take your diving to another level, and are intrigued by underwater environments, then you might want to learn a little about ice diving – see IDEA 3, *Solid sky*.

Defining idea...

'*Cave diving calls for complete self-reliance and independence of judgement, which does not imply ignoring the experience of others. The diver's responsibility for safety is his and his alone. He [or she] must to a great extent live cave diving as well as practice it.*'
From the manual of the *Cave Diving Group of Great Britain*

How did it go?

Q **I am interested in trying cave diving and took a cavern diver speciality course but had real trouble with the buoyancy aspect and was told by the instructor that I wasn't good enough to be trusted in a fragile or silty environment yet. Now what?**

A *Back to basics. Buoyancy in any overhead diving environment is essential so rather than spend a lot of money on cave/cavern-specific instruction go back to a bog-standard dive centre and ask to do a peak performance buoyancy course (or equivalent). Such courses usually take place in a pool and just focus on buoyancy, with plenty of tips and tricks, so you can focus on getting that just right before you venture into overhead environments.*

Q **I have a lot of wreck-penetration diving experience (and qualifications) – what else would I need to learn to cave dive?**

A *You will need to work on your navigation (especially blind navigation), guideline and rope work (bet you never learnt to abseil in order to wreck dive). Buoyancy is a key skill as just one misplaced kick into a silt bottom may mean you have to abort a dive. Finally, there is a lot of equipment to get used to; many cave divers use a system of built-in redundant regulators and on/off controls that you probably won't have seen before. There is no doubt, however, that wreck-penetration skills will stand you in good stead for your next step.*

9

Surfing on snow

For reasons probably best known to marketing people, snowboarding is probably the 'coolest' sport outside of surfing in Hawaii. Don't let that put you off.

You don't have to know what 'shredding' means to have a ball.

You can always tell a board-sports virgin by the look they give you when you ask them if they're 'goofy' or 'regular'. Deciding which foot you favour is the first step towards any kind of boarding so don't be too surprised if your first lesson in snowboarding consists of being lined up with other likely suspects and then given a shove. Whichever foot you instinctively put out to stop yourself falling will define your boarding forever more. If it's your left foot then you're 'goofy', by the way, which means a) you will ride right foot forwards, and b) you will need the patience to put up with feeble jokes every time you encounter a total novice who has just learned what goofy and regular are.

Once bound in you should first make a little platform in the snow, perpendicular to the slope to balance the board on as you stand up. Otherwise you're going to start sliding before you mean to. Moving is easy – just hop up in the air and land so you're pointing down the slope and you'll be away. Terrified, out of control and about to fall over, but away nonetheless.

Here's an idea for you...

Get your skates on. 'Skating' is the technique for pushing yourself along the ground on the flat. Since most new boarders are busy focusing on how to stop and turn they forget this simple skill and hordes of them only find out how essential it is as they try to use a chairlift for the first time. Whether you ride goofy or regular you'll want to unclip the back foot to push, as pushing with the front foot (pushing 'mongo' as skateboarders say) is harder work and more likely to tip you over right in front of the chairlift queue. You'll notice there's a friction pad between the front and back bindings. That's called the stomp plate and it's where you place your free foot as you glide in skate mode. Practise the skating before you even think of going near that chairlift and then you can afford to chortle as your mates penguin, wobble and wipeout before they even reach the slope.

Just in case you actually wanted to be in control you're going to have to master a couple of the basics. Start with the heelside (also called the backside – it's the edge nearest your heels) slide. Standing on your little platform look down the slope and point the toes on both feet. You will start to slide down the hill. Just before you turn into a human snowball try pulling both sets of toes back up. You should slow and stop. Now we're getting somewhere.

Next start off as before and just press down with the toes of your front foot (left foot if you're regular). You should slide down but also across the run; as you get to the other side pull up with that foot and start to press down with the toes of the other foot. This way you should describe a series of zigzags down the slope, facing forward all the time. Pull back with both toes at the bottom and you've completed your first run.

Now try the same thing with the toeside (front) edge. For the toeside slide you need to do the reverse – pushing down with the *heel* of your lead foot. From there you go to heelsiding until you're facing down the slope (panic, panic, panic) then pull up the toes to turn away – only now you try and join it all up by going into a toeside slide. Get it right and you will carve curves all the way down. At which point you are shredding, dude/dudette/madam dude.

If snowboarding is a little too much to learn in one go then try sandboarding – IDEA 31, *Circles in the sand*.

Try another idea...

From then on you only have to remember that a snowboard works much like a ski. As you tilt it, one edge cuts into the snow like a knife. If you exert pressure in the middle of the board it bows and that turns into an arc. Boards for freestyle (tricks) are bendier so they can turn sharper turns and perform more tricks. Alpine and racing boards are stiffer and offer more control at higher speeds. Likewise, freestyle boots are those nice-looking soft jobs and Alpine boots are unmistakeably mutant ski boots. Do bear that in mind when choosing gear, rather than just going for the comfy option.

'I now realize that the small hills you see on ski slopes are formed around the bodies of 47-year-olds who tried to learn snowboarding.'
DAVE BARRY, American writer and humorist

Defining idea...

35

How did it go?

Q   Erm, what does 'shredding' actually mean?

A   *Fair question. It means riding fast and stylishly.*

Q   I am wiping out fast and frequently and it is killing my hands more than anything else, any ideas?

A   *It may not look too cool but if you get into the habit of balling up your hands into fists as you build speed you will probably save yourself a lot of wrenched fingers and thumbs from the temptation to put a hand out with every speed wobble.*

Q   Why can't I get the damn bindings off so I can walk off the ski lifts?

A   *Normal ski bindings have a quick release so you don't break your pelvis as one leg goes one way and the other wraps itself around your neck. That's not a risk with a snowboard and, believe it or not, your best bet for avoiding being split like a turkey wishbone lies in binding both legs together. Fixing them to the board is the easiest way of doing that, so we put up with the awkwardness as a way of saving ourselves from worse.*

10

An elephant can do it

Gleaming motorboats, smiles, suntans and the rush of skis swishing over the water effortlessly carving elegant semi-circles in their wake...

Waterskiing is the epitome of Riviera chic — as long as you can actually stand up, that is.

Back when Santa Monica's Muscle Beach was establishing itself as the focus of fitness there used to be a lady called Paula Boelsems who made her living showing her waterskiing elephant. Amusing and harmless, you might think, except that ever since it has been used by waterski savvy 'mates' to taunt those of us whose principal sporting talent consists of falling off things. 'How hard can it be?' they chorus. 'You only have to stand up, and besides, an elephant can do it.'

So you end up agreeing to having a go. You don the gear, buckle up the flotation vest and get ready, all the time thinking 'all I have to do is stand up, all I have to do is stand up'. Then the driver guns the engine, the motorboat roars off and you take a short flight, overtaking your skis and nosediving into the water, hopefully losing the rope in the process ... otherwise you're about to look like an extra from a watery version of *Ben Hur* as you get dragged, hurtling and howling, through the spray.

Here's an idea for you...

So: you can get to your feet, you can ride over the wake without being spat off the line, and you're starting to eye up those ramps over there. Before you do, just try feeling the speed by carving big circles around the outside of the boat. Try and overtake it. You can't, obviously, but by forgetting about being towed directly behind it and instead arcing out to the side you can come close to drawing level with the boat, at which point the tension on the line and the feeling of speed are considerable. It's also the first step towards taking a jump, so get used to the feeling.

What you've probably done is focus so hard on the idea of standing up that you've tried to get upright by means of your own muscles. After all, that's what you've been doing ever since you were a toddler so it's a hard habit to break. Well, don't. You've paid to be hitched up to a high-speed motorboat so let it do all the work of getting you upright – leaving your own muscles free to concentrate on maintaining your body position. When you're in the water keep the knees bent but strong, and likewise brace your arms but don't lock out the elbows. The reason is that your limbs need that little bit of elasticity to deal with the forces coming their way and locked legs and arms give you no flexibility. As the boat pulls, let the planing motion of the skis be the force that lifts you out of the water. Don't even think about standing up, just concentrate on keeping your legs strong and bent. Oh sure, you may not look overly elegant: in fact, with your bottom sticking out one way, your body hunched over and your forehead furrowed in concentration you will look like a Neanderthal that has accidentally harpooned something way too big to handle – but at least you won't be nosediving. The truth is that standing up is something you can safely leave until you are well and truly out of the water and riding high.

At the same time keep a grip on the handle but resist the desire to pull it towards you. Pull on the rope and you are engaged in a tug of war with a roaring speedboat. Instead keep your shoulders right back, push your chest out forward and keep your arms strong so that the rope isn't yanked out of your hands as the boat moves off. Having locked elbows makes it easier for the rope to break your grip so keep your elbows flexed but flexible. Remember that if you do let go of the rope it will go pinging off straight at your mates in the boat which may make them think twice about coming back to give you another go. If your legs aren't strong and tensed then you will simply be pulled over forwards which means you are going to nosedive. Remember the tug of war and get ready to take the strain.

If it's tricks you're after on the water then take a look at wakeboarding in IDEA 37, *Eat my wake*.

Try another idea...

When you're up you will probably just be happy to stay there and feel the rush of skimming over the water's surface. Which is what it's all about, after all. Do try, however, to get used to a little bumpy stuff by going over the wake of the boat. You can't avoid it forever and your driver may give you no option anyway, maybe turning to avoid hitting objects or running out of water. Keep those legs and arms flexed but flexible and you'll overcome that feeling of driving over a ploughed field.

'It's hard for the modern generation to understand Thoreau, who lived beside a pond but didn't own waterskis or a snorkel.'
BILL VAUGHN, American author and mentor

Defining idea...

How did it go?

Q **The skis actually seem to sink beneath me as I start, resulting in a nifty submarine impression. Why?**

A *You're probably standing up too early and pointing the skis downwards in the process. Don't worry about standing up at all, let the boat bring you up, still crouched if necessary.*

Q **My legs are cast iron, my shoulders are so far back my shoulder blades nearly meet and yet I'm still tipping over forwards and going snorkelling instead of skiing. Any ideas?**

A *Are you pulling the handle in towards your navel without realising it? Pulling the rope towards you is likely to destabilise you anyway, and if you pull it down low then it becomes more likely that your head will overtake it and you will cartwheel.*

11

This is a raid!

The Raid World Championship, Eco Challenge and Coast to Coast represent the extreme of adventure racing.

This is the point at which expedition and competition come together in a cross between sport and survival.

Modestly billed as 'the toughest and most dangerous adventure race in the world', the Raid Gauloises kicked off in New Zealand at the end of the 80s. While it was not the first extreme adventure race (it was predated by the likes of the Coast to Coast – also in New Zealand) it was better publicised than most, and can be argued to be the point at which adventure racing went from a local event for hardy fanatics to become a televised global sport. Perhaps appropriately enough the Raid Gauloises has since evolved into the Raid World Championship, and its logo has been adorned with the ubiquitous 'X' for extreme.

The use of the word 'raid' is confusing because it means many things to many people – including the French. Usually taken to mean a 'foray' or 'expedition' the word is used in France to describe a large number of multi-day races, including all multi-stage races on foot (such as the famous Marathon des Sables in the Sahara).

Here's an idea for you...

Multi-day, multidiscipline events are about a lot more than athletic ability. However much you might train for individual legs by running or cycling the event is ultimately less about 'racing' and more about self-management. Obviously, that means taking care of your body with proper nutrition, hydration and blister care, but it also means keeping a close eye on your emotional ride, and a very large part of that is learning to live with less sleep. One of the top tips for this is learning to power nap – the art of lying (or sitting down), shutting your eyes and sleeping for half an hour here or there to rapidly recharge your batteries. Since not many of us do this normally, it means getting into the habit during your training.

Largely thanks to the original Raid Gauloises, however, the English-speaking world uses the term to describe multi-day wilderness races, usually using a variety of disciplines ranging from snowshoes to canoes. There are any number of raids around the world (try www.sleepmonsters.com for a few ideas) but the best known are the Eco Challenge and the Raid World Championship. A look at them will give you an idea of what to expect.

ECO CHALLENGE

Originally New Zealand endurance races lasted a day or two. The famous Coast to Coast starts at dawn with one foot in the Tasman Sea and, after 250 km or so of paddling, cycling and running, finishes at the Pacific Ocean. Back in 1992, Mark Burnett looked at this model and lengthened the race, removed any assistance crews and added a strong environmental message, thereby creating the Eco Challenge. The Eco Challenge claims to be 'the world's toughest Expedition Race', describing itself (not unreasonably) as 'epic, gritty and unpredictable'. As you may have guessed, the Eco Challenge and Raid Gauloises found themselves locked in an instant media rivalry.

Each Eco Challenge team consists of four with at least one man or woman per team. They race non-stop, twenty-four hours a day, over a rugged 500 km (300 mile) course, participating in such disciplines as trekking, white-water canoeing, horseback riding, sea kayaking, scuba diving, mountaineering and mountain biking. It's enough to make you tired just reading about it. The location changes every year and it's not uncommon to have to be helicoptered to the start, never mind out again if anything goes awry.

THE RAID WORLD CHAMPIONSHIP

In a bid to go one up on the Eco Challenge and establish itself as 'the reference' for adventure racing, this now features the best teams from five continents, qualifying by means of the X-adventure Raid Series. It too is a non-stop, long-distance raid lasting five to seven days and features disciplines ranging from snowshoe racing to in-line skating, sea kayaking, crampons and caving.

Try another idea...

If you like the idea of this kind of extreme but don't think you're quite up to the level required then don't worry – the big boys have spun off plenty of shorter, 'taster' events, some lasting only a few hours. Take a look at IDEA 7, *A taste for adventure.*

Defining idea...

'I am often asked what qualities are needed to make a person successful at such difficult undertakings. My answer is always the same and often surprises people. I firmly believe that one does not need to be particularly brave, strong or even foolhardy; instead you need a very defective short-term memory.'
MIKE STROUD, competitor in one of the first Eco Challenges, explorer and author of *Survival of the Fittest*

45

How did it go?

Q **At some point there is always climbing or abseiling to do and I find that while I am just great at it in the climbing gym I am all over the shop when I have to do it wearing a rucksack in the event. Any suggestions?**

A *Try slinging your rucksack very low down your back or under your bottom as it will help keep you upright during rope work rather than trying to flip you over. If that still doesn't work then you may want to think about persuading the strongest member of the team to carry it for you.*

Q **I have difficulty husbanding my energy – I seem to exhaust myself in some stages and then relax so much in others (notably canoeing) that I drop off to sleep. Aside from practising more, is there anything I can do?**

A *Sounds like you need to have a third-party pace setter. That can be another member of the team, to whom you need to give the authority to tell you when to slow down/speed up, or it could be a heart monitor. A heart monitor is the easiest as you can set yourself training zones with alarms when you go above or below them. That way as you overdo it, or start to take it too easy, the little swine will bleep naggingly at you.*

12

Catching waves

First the good news: you don't have to have tribal tattoos, a washboard stomach and blond highlights to become a surfer...

Now the bad news: you're going to fall off. Lots.

For some people life is about making a living and founding a family. For others it is all about trying to stand upright on a plastic plank while Mother Nature does her level best to hurl you upside down into the primeval sea as if reproaching you for having had the impertinence to crawl out of it in the first place. Anyone who hasn't spent the last forty years living under a rock can tell you that surfing is implausibly glamorous, hip and heavily marketed. It's as if everyone who has ever thought 'hmm, yes I do look pretty nifty in Speedos' has immediately been signed up by some all-seeing surfing talent scout.

What's fascinating, however, is that for every bronzed beach-god sunning themselves in the Hawaiian surf there will also be a bedraggled bloke shivering in a car park in Wales. Take away the glamour, the suntans, the fashion statements and the groupies (or so I'm told) and people will still follow the surf with a zeal verging on religious mania. That alone makes it worth a whirl.

Here's an idea for you...

When you first fling yourself onto your board and start paddling to catch a wave the chances are that you will feel unbalanced and tip from side to side or find yourself too far back down the board so the nose rises up from the water (a common mistake called 'corking'). Then you'll unbalance further as you shift your weight around trying to find the neutral spot, only to be taken unawares as the wave catches you and passes you by. Save time and hassle by starting off in flat water, lying on the board so that it floats flat. Then mark where your shoulders and chin go on the board with surf wax (so you can wipe it off later). Now, when you try to catch waves, you already have a body outline to line up with as you take your place on the board.

Surfing started out way before the Beach Boys and was probably once the preserve of the natives of Hawaii. Denizens of Hawaii will tell you that surfing is a near-mystical experience in which you become 'one with the wave'. Those of us who first wet our wax in less glamorous locations can assure you that it is easy to become one with the wave but that's only because you tend to disappear into it the moment you try to get to your feet. So let's get real. Surfing is fun to try, and don't whatever you do be put off by the too-cool-for-school image of it, but on the other hand it's not a half day on a beginner's board that is going to transform you into Laird Hamilton (whaddya mean 'who?'!).

SURF'S UP

First, don't just rush into the waves with the nearest board to hand. If you haven't done this before then make sure you have professionals to keep an eye on you and ask if they have 'soft' boards before you agree to go. Soft boards are more like hard foam. They are less glamorous, they don't perform as well and you can't hang around rubbing wax on them and looking cool because they aren't even shiny. What they are, however, is, erm, soft. Well, softer than the real thing anyway and when you've been banged around the head by a wave brandishing your own board you start to appreciate that kind of detail.

Mastering the waves is only half way there – try mastering sea and sky at the same time with IDEA 45, *Windsurfing*.*Try another idea...*

Practice your 'snap' in easy waves. Bring your hand up to your ribcage, lift your head and shoulders up and then snap your right foot (presuming you're not left-footed) straight up under you so that your chest is resting on your knee. Now turn both feet sideways so they face across the board and you are up. Keep nice and low and stick your bottom out as far as it'll go. Now get out there and do much the same thing. You'll fall off of the first forty or fifty times, but the first time you are up for even a couple of seconds your friends won't be able to shut you up about it.

SO WHERE DO I GO FROM HERE?

Once you've mastered the basics the sky's the limit. Literally. Sure, there are moves like the floater or the tailside (dude), but it's the aerial that wows the crowds. An aptly-named man called Christian Fletcher is credited as the mutineer who brought skateboarding moves to surfing and 'wasted' the best part of the wave by using it for take-off instead of riding it. You need to build speed by racing down the face of the wave then up to the lip to take-off and catch some air. It doesn't count if you don't land upright, by the way: that's not called an aerial, just a spectacular wipeout.

'Until you actually paddle out onto a wave you'll never know what it's like. It's the most fantastic feeling to be with the ocean.'
CHERON KRAAK, surfer (and CEO Billabong SA)

Defining idea...

STILL NOT ENOUGH FOR YOU?

Right then, surf-god Laird Hamilton invented tow-in surfing, where a jetski tows the surfer right into high-speed, monster waves that paddlers could never catch. Beat that.

How did it go? **Q   I never seem to catch the wave – I paddle like a mad thing and they just pass me by. Why?**

A   *Could be you're not paddling well enough. Never paddle with both arms together – instead go for a front crawl but, unlike swimming, try cupping your hands to grab as much water as you can.*

Q   I just can't get up and I'm getting disheartened. What now?

A   *As a hardened expert in the art of falling off things I know just where you're coming from, but go back and practise on land before you give up. Draw an imaginary surfboard on the sand and lie on its centreline. Then have a friend tell you to snap and criticise your speed and end position.*

13

Back to basics – BASE jumping

Jumping off something, with only a few seconds freefall between yourself and a landing spot that could be cluttered with trees, cars or cattle, isn't an activity you'll find on your next adventure holiday.

For a select few, however, it is the ultimate sport.

BASE stands for Building, Antenna, Span (bridge), Earth (usually a cliff) and represents the four main types of jump for a full BASE jumper. When BASE jumping started up in 1981 the founding fathers of the sport had to complete jumps in all four categories before being assigned their BASE number. For the record, Phil Smith of Houston, Texas is BASE number one. While jumping off a fixed object has been around since the first jumps from tethered balloons, the sport today came from the realisation that square canopies opened faster and could be steered more accurately to get away from the start point and (hopefully) towards a safe landing point.

A lot of the early jumps were done from the El Capitan cliff in the US and one of the turning points was the day when canopy design enabled jumpers to clear the trees

Here's an idea for you...

Not got the full number of jumps but think you're ready for it? Well then, make your way to Bridge Day, the largest BASE jumping event in the world, held in October every year in Fayetteville, West Virginia. Hundreds of BASE jumpers gather to launch (legally) from the New River Gorge Bridge and there are two days of seminars on technique. For your first BASE jump you need only fifty parachute jumps plus a suitable chute and the right attitude (if they don't think you have it then you'll have to wait until next year). There is nothing else like it. Full details and registration from www.bridgeday.info.

below and reach a nearby meadow for landing. Unfortunately El Capitan is situated in Yosemite National Park and this led to a falling out with park authorities that is often seen as the beginning of BASE jumping's messy legal status worldwide. BASE jumping itself isn't illegal, but there are no end of trespass and safety laws that it can infringe and many a successful jump has ended with the jumper being taken into custody. Of course, that has added an outlaw image to the sport which has helped popularise it. Certainly it has a slightly underground culture and is probably practised by only a couple of thousand people worldwide, though there is no way of knowing how many try it once and then think better of it.

The essential problem is that the margins of error involved are minimal. Heights are at the very edge of even the best canopy's ability to deploy and be steered away from the ground. Pilot chutes (to pull open the main chute) usually have to be deployed by hand at the split second of jumping in order to have a chance of opening and, even when safely opened, the problems of other objects such as antennae or buildings still have to be negotiated. Nick Di Giovanni (BASE 194), maintains a BASE jumping fatality list which at time of writing lists eighty-four jumpers who didn't make it. In a sport with so few participants that's not good news.

That said, there is no denying the beauty of some of those death-defying leaps and watching BASE jumpers soaring from the heights of Angel Falls or the Kuala Lumpur tower is dizzying and inspiring.

Not so extreme but every bit as technically challenging is sky surfing – see IDEA 43, *Freefall fandango*.

Try another idea...

So what can you do if you're hell-bent on BASE? The general advice is that you shouldn't even think about it until you have 150 freefall jumps under your belt, but if you have notched up the jumps and can't fight the urge to BASE jump then at least go about it sensibly. For a start, search out others who have already done it and see if you can learn at their feet. Offer your help in any way you can but don't become a pain and remember that a student may be seen as nothing more than a liability by people who have enough to worry about already. Conventional wisdom is that you'll need to focus on your jump accuracy and as many different landing approaches as you can, preferably using a seven-cell canopy. Learn everything there is to know about packing and rigging – some manufacturers offer courses and there's no doubt that you will learn better, and with fewer risks, under the eyes of a company with a vested interest in your succeeding. Most such manufacturers are in the States but if you're daunted by the idea of travelling for your sport then you might want to take up Xtreme tiddlywinks instead. Planning on developing and practicing BASE jumping entirely in one location is unlikely to get you far and if you want to become one of a select few you will have to make sacrifices for your sport.

'We'll jump off that bridge when we come to it.'
BASE jumper's motto

Defining idea...

How did
it go?

Q How do I go about meeting other BASE jumpers to find out more?

A *All BASE jumpers are also parachutists and if you join a club or hang around a drop zone long enough you will find yourself in the company of BASE jumpers sooner or later.*

Q Can I use my skydiving canopy?

A *There is a school of thought that says that many skydiving canopies have unsuitable speed/performance and braking characteristics. There are such things as BASE-specific canopies (such as Consolidated Rigging's 'Mojo') but it is equally true that BASE jumping has been done with pretty much everything including old-fashioned round canopies before now. If you're serious enough to think about a dedicated canopy then you should know enough other practitioners to compare notes.*

14

Getting the hang of it

Soaring suspended beneath a thin rigid wing is the stuff of dreams. Paragliding may have brought silent flight to the masses, but for pure performance hang gliders still have the edge.

Where there is a cliff, a stiff breeze and some sun you will see people making mankind's oldest dream come true by soaring like the birds.

These days most of those flyers will be paragliders, since the portability and ease of paragliding makes it a more obvious choice for beginners. A select few, however, will be hanging horizontally, slung beneath the sleek delta wings of hang gliders. So what's the difference? Ask a paraglider pilot and they will point out that hang gliders take longer to master, can't be packed into a backpack and usually require a car to transport. Ask a hang-gliding pilot and they will tell you that hang gliders are far faster, with superior gliding characteristics and the ability to fly in stronger wind. Which may explain why you are more likely to see hang gliders in the brisk breezes of the Sussex cliffs and paragliders in the soft winds of the tropics.

Here's an idea for you...

To get an idea of whether hang gliding is for you it is not necessary to put yourself through a ten-day course. There are taster courses which give you a basic introduction and have you performing short skims (as far as I'm concerned when your feet are off the ground you're flying) In a day or so. Better yet, sign up for a tandem flight where you will be in a sling alongside the instructor so you not only get to fly but can listen to the explanations of how to control the wing, without the responsibility of flying/crashing it yourself.

Partisans of both approaches will argue until they are blue in the face about which is the safest. Probably the best approach is to remember the original story of flying man, in which Icarus ended up tumbling out of the sky. What's often forgotten in that tale is that Icarus was not alone in the sky and that his father Daedalus completed his flight successfully. The moral of the story is that it is the pilot, more often than the craft, that defines the risk factor.

Learning to hang glide takes a week to ten days to get up to a basic level where you are free to join clubs or turn up at popular sites and launch your own craft. Flying requires very little strength because you hang from a sling, not from your arms, but launching is tiring because you have to jog along with 35 kg of glider on your shoulders. This means that the first week is probably the most tiring part of your flying career. You'll have company, though, since the instructor is going to have to jog alongside you over and over as you go through dummy launches.

You will progress to low skimming flights, 30° turns (you turn by shifting your weight to the side or forwards/backwards in the harness), and then off the training gliders onto higher-performance craft and higher flights. You'll need to show the ability to perform a 180° controlled turn and land where you're told to – which involves a process called 'flaring', essentially stalling the wing just as you want to stop. Finally you'll have to pass a theory exam covering the law and physics of flying as well as the basics of navigation. Navigation? Well, yes: you can end up travelling a fair old way. The current record flights are over the 700 km mark, and while altitude is often governed by the airspace regulations of the country you are in, flights can reach 4800 m or more when the pilots are equipped with oxygen. Which makes it more of a budget airline than a sport.

If you love unpowered flight, but want to learn faster and have more flexibility about where you can launch from, then perhaps you should look at IDEA 32, *Paragliding*.

Try another idea...

The trick to long distance and altitude is reading the air's behaviour. As with any gliding you will be looking for thermals, places where a column of warmer air rises. These occur anywhere that patches of ground absorb heat faster than their surroundings, including car parks, tarmac roads or rocks surrounded by grass. The other major source of lift is known as ridge lift and occurs where wind blows onto a cliff or hill and is forced up the face so that it goes upwards, creating a wall of rising air and enabling a technique called ridge soaring. Put simply, thermals enable cross-country flying, and ridge lift is what allows pilots to hang seemingly motionless above the ground looking out to sea, like gulls.

'Once you have tasted flight, you will walk the earth with your eyes turned forever skyward, for there you have been, and there you long to return.'
LEONARDO DA VINCI, father of hang gliding

Defining idea...

How did it go?

Q **I'd love to but I'm afraid of heights, what chance have I got?**

A *Try it – seriously. It's a little hard to explain but you will feel less vertigo when suspended in plain air than when looking down from a building with reference points that tell you how high up you are.*

Q **Can I carry a parachute?**

A *Yes indeedy. In fact all hang-glider pilots fly with a parachute attached to their harness.*

Q **I'm a woman. Will I be strong enough?**

A *Remember that it is the sling, rather than your upper body, that takes the weight. A lot of instructors comment on the fact that women make excellent pilots, often better pilots than the men.*

15

Swimming up solid water – ice climbing

Climbing ice is like nothing else on earth.

Aside from being slippery, cold and easily shattered, ice is in a constant state of change and the fast-rising sun behind you means you are against the clock as you scale that freezing face.

Even the climbers themselves are quick to point out the downside of their sport. They joke about preparing for it by sitting in the fridge or beating themselves around the body with a frozen leg of lamb. Stories abound about the dangers of climbing cliffs that are only temporarily solid. Of ice breaking away and tumbling, or the sphincter-tightening realisation that beneath the frozen waterfall you are scaling there is a very live, wet and active waterfall trying to get out.

Yet ice climbers are often near fanatical in their devotion to what would seem a notably dangerous and uncomfortable sport. In part that's down to the sheer beauty of the element itself. Ice glistens and refracts the light, it comes in many colours from pure whites to green and the startling aquamarines of glaciers. Climbing a frozen waterfall is a fairytale moment, with the sensation that at any time the spell could be broken and the ice will revert to playing water. Plus there's

Here's an idea for you...

One of the classic mistakes when starting out is to think that the safest way of bedding an ice axe into the ice is to take a swing at it like an executioner beheading royalty. Guys in particular are prone to beginning their ascent with a series of almighty thwacks, at least until their arms fill with lactic acid and feel like lead. In fact, the sledgehammer approach may even fracture the ice and make it harder – so before going at it hammer and tongs try to read the 'flow' of the ice and focus more on getting the angle right so the axe bites, rather than expecting brute force to do the job.

what has been called the 'Spiderman' factor, as you make your way up seemingly glass-like faces thanks to a pair of ice axes tethered to your arms, and the points of your crampon-shod tootsies.

Ice climbing isn't something you can go and try without supervision. Apart from the dangers posed by the ice itself there are plenty that you can come up with all by yourself when you have a razor-sharp axe in each hand and a set of spikes on each foot. It's a common joke that you can pick out an ice climber by the neat adze (the back point of the axe) scars on the forehead from where they've whacked themselves in the face pulling a reluctant axe out of the ice.

Get thee to an ice climbing school and your teachers will a) tell you jokes about fridges and frozen cuts of meat, b) take you to a good spot for beginners, either a small wall of ice (often a frozen waterfall) or else a more gentle gradient on which to get going. From there you are going to have to get used to the viciously sharp bits of hardware that are attached to your body. A common first lesson is using the ice axe to stop yourself sliding off the mountain if you fall over. This will involve a lot of falling over in the snow so if you haven't dressed the part you aren't going to go the distance. When you fall the idea is to roll over onto your front and dig the axe into the ground so it acts as an anchor and stops your slide. The faster you make that move the less speed you build up before braking and the more effective it is, so the idea is that it should become an instant reflex.

Once you've got the hang of that it's time to get vertical and that involves the two principal approaches to placing your feet. Beginners normally start with the 'pied à plat' (flat foot) style of planting the entire sole of the foot against the ice face to get a grip. It makes sense but since your body is parallel, rather than perpendicular, to that ice face the whole process involves some ankle-dislocating moves like a game of Twister, only upright and with added spikes. The alternative is jamming only the front spikes of the toes into the ice face – a move that requires a lot more self-confidence. The idea is to work axes and crampons together so that you are always anchored at three points before you try and place the fourth. In addition to that you have another layer of protection in the form of ice screws, which screw into the ice much as cams are used to protect trad climbers on rock. With the important difference that rock protections are solid and ice protections are, well, dicey.

So why do it? Ask anyone who has made it to the top of even the smallest of ice walls, and sat out of breath and sweaty at the top, looking at the light glancing off the glistening surface. They'll tell you they've never felt happier in their whole life.

Prefer to get the hang of scaling something more solid than temporarily thick water? Try *Rad tradding* – IDEA 35.

Try another idea…

'*It's snowing still,' said Eeyore gloomily. 'So it is.' 'And freezing.' 'Is it?' 'Yes,' said Eeyore. 'However,' he said, brightening up a little, 'we haven't had an earthquake lately.'*
A.A. MILNE

Defining idea…

Q **Do I need boots or will trainers do?**

A *Would you ski in trainers? Aside from the risk of twisting your ankle, you need a shoe that crampons can lock on to and trainers just won't cut it.*

Q **What if my axes and crampons slip?**

A *You'll be on belay, meaning your instructor has you on a safety rope which runs up to a fixed point above you and back down to you. Even if you decide to do a 'Superman', your instructor will be able to hold you.*

16

Bailing out

Throwing yourself out of an aeroplane is normally considered a last option rather than a first choice, but the demand for parachuting courses amounts to a positive freefall frenzy.

Here are some options for how to go about it.

Whether you're looking to act out that paratrooper fantasy, recreate James Bond's freefalling acrobatics or just put yourself through the joyride of a lifetime then parachuting, and its close cousin freefalling, are available somewhere near you – wherever you live. To get into parachuting today there are basically two ways to go.

TANDEM

If you don't really see yourself parachuting regularly in the future, and just want a white-knuckle freefall frenzy, then a tandem dive is unquestionably for you. For a tandem jump you are given a ten-minute briefing on what's expected of you (precious little), and that's it. You're then strapped to the instructor who has a larger than average parachute so he/she does all the work and you just enjoy the ride. You will take off in a plane that looks like something bought second-hand from the Red Baron, shout a few pleasantries to the instructor, and then pitch out of the door. By the time you've opened your eyes you'll be freefalling at about 200 km/h before the instructor pulls the cord and guides you smoothly down for a few minutes of parachuting.

Here's an idea for you... **Whether you're a beginner who knows you are never going to do this again, or on the way to becoming a full-on Skydiving God, you can learn a lot from watching what you did as you fell. A lot of operators and clubs can arrange a video cameraman/woman (they jump with you and film using a helmet-mounted camera) to capture every detail, so shop around and find out who can capture your freefall for all time.**

STATIC LINE

Static-line jumping takes a little more input on your part, and requires a bit more time, but is typically a lot cheaper because you don't require an instructor physically attached to you. Typically an operator will offer the static-line jump course all in one day, with the morning taken up with tuition. The meat of that consists of landings so you can expect to practise forward, backward and sideways jumps off a step or box and onto a mat until you are sick of it and the instructor is happy. At which point you will probably be asked to lie flat on your belly with your arms and legs stuck out and practise counting aloud before checking your canopy. Then in the afternoon you'll be bundled into the Boeing Biggles as usual and shoved out the door. The point of a static-line jump is that your main chute is hooked up to the plane so that it is pulled automatically as you leave the plane, hence all you should have to do is adopt the position and wait for it to deploy. After that you drift gently down until you meet the land and that's it: you have completed your first jump.

From there on it's downhill all the way, because your next step, one way or another, is freefall.

FREEFALL FRENZY

The downside of static-line jumping is that you don't really savour freefall (discounting the seconds taken for the chute to open) and nor will you until you have completed five to ten more static-line jumps, working up to full freefall with tasks such as pulling dummy ripcords as you go. While the process varies from place to place it is not unusual to take forty to fifty jumps before you are qualified to freefall through the classic route.

Want to take it a step further? Once you're qualified as a freefaller you can get creative with sky surfing or so called 'relative' manoeuvres (synchronised sky surfing, really) – see IDEA 43, *Freefall fandango*.

Try another idea...

AFF

There is, however, a quicker way. AFF, or Accelerated Free Fall, is the fast track to freefall for those determined to get their 'A' Licence (the international freefall qualification) in a hurry. You still start with a static-line jump but your very next outing will be your first full-on freefall. If you're wondering how on earth you make that particular leap of faith the answer is simple – you will have two instructors literally holding your hand (or anything else they see fit to grab) as you go. You will have to open your own chute, but they'll take you through the whole thing with sign language and hopefully see fit to save your life if you turn out to be a potentially terminal muppet. From there on you move through different levels of training, focusing on your directional skills

'Life changed after that jump ... I'd suddenly stepped to the highest level of daring, a level above even that which airplane pilots could attain.'
CHARLES A. LINDBERGH, describing his first jump

Defining idea...

69

and stability and introducing more advanced moves and, finally, low-altitude opening. As you advance, the number of hand-holders drops off from two to one until you are being observed in a hands-off mode. Getting to the point where you are jumping and freefalling without anyone else laying a finger on can take as little as a few days. You still have to clock up the minimum twenty-five jumps for your 'A' licence, but weather permitting you can go through the whole thing from start to finish in weeks rather than months.

How did it go?

Q   I fancy a tandem jump but I'm the size of Schwarzenneger – is this a problem?

A   Could be. Some operators impose a top limit on weight (typically around 105 kg) but they may be flexible depending on the parachutes and instructors available – what you must do is call well in advance and explain your situation so they can try and accommodate you.

Q   I'm curious about static line, but what if I freeze when it's my turn to jump?

A   There are a lot of macho stories about jumpmasters shoving terrified individuals out of the plane but in reality reputable operators and clubs aren't going to do that – even though your chute will open regardless, you may not have the wherewithal to land properly and so are more likely to hurt yourself (and sue).

17

Just for the heli of it – heli skiing

Anyone who's ever been dazzled by the pristine glister of fresh snow can appreciate the beauty of skiing a virgin run, far from the madding crowd.

Add the adrenaline of a helicopter flight to find that location and you have a heady sporting mix indeed.

There used to be a TV ad for a brand of chocolates that featured an anonymous hero leaping out of helicopters and skiing through avalanches in order to deliver a box of chocs to his lady love. Like you do. For me heli skiing still has precisely that same aura of improbable glamour; if it didn't exist an ad agency would have made it up. Those who have taken the whirlybird route to off-piste paradise will rave about pristine powder, and breathtaking vistas until they start to dribble. Hardcore technical types will reel off 'vertical metre' stats like telephone numbers – some will guarantee you 20,000 vertical metres in six days. Heli ski routes often feature single runs higher than the summits of the mountains in popular ski resorts.

Here's an idea for you...

Heli skiing hurts. Right in the wallet. So how about a halfway house that gets you off the beaten track but doesn't take a second mortgage to finance? That's the idea behind 'cat' skiing. The cat in question is a snowcat: a tracked vehicle that trundles up the snow faces to take you away from it all and then back down to pick you up ready for another go. Snowcats offer one of the cheapest ways of getting out onto virgin powder, travel far and wide to find snow, are never grounded by mist and would be hard pushed to tumble out of the sky.

Of course, it doesn't hurt that the locations suited for heli skiing are without exception gloriously spectacular and remote. Popular choices include the Himalayas, Alaska, Canada, Greenland and the Kamchatka peninsula of Russia. Close your eyes and you can almost picture yourself there. While you're at it you may also be able to hear a faint whining noise like an animal in pain. That'll be your bank manager.

Heli skiing is not cheap. While some operators use helicopters able to carry groups of up to ten, a lot more fly smaller craft with groups of four or five on board. Which means that a mere handful of you are chartering a private flight with a specialist pilot. It's not exactly a question of 'if you have to ask the price you can't afford it', but a week's heli skiing in Kamchatka, for example, is likely to cost you over $3000 for accommodation and chopper rides alone. If you're not sure then look for places that offer weekend packages rather than the full week. If you're a European who chooses to snow in Aspen, or an American who opts to snow in Europe, then the cost might not seem quite so exorbitant. Plus you can always console yourself with the thought that you're getting an experience normally only available by joining the marines and being posted to Norway. And you don't even have to get the tattoos.

There is also a small issue of ability. You don't want to find that your powder skills aren't really up to it when you're 3000 metres up and the only ski lift is disappearing noisily into the distance. Heli skiing is for skiers and snowboarders who are already confident off-piste and in varying weather. The guides will be there to help you, but if something goes wrong you are a long way from backup so you have to be prepared to get yourself out of whatever you get yourself into. Recommended skills include side-step uphill, traversing and kick turns for both skiers and boarders. Less technical but no less important is the ability to do what you're told – if the guide tells you to keep to the left, you keep to the left. Be aware that there will also be pressure to keep up because more than one group may share a helicopter and they will only be allowed to progress as fast as the weakest skier. That said, some operators go out of their way to cater for the less hardcore – those who might be comfortable with black runs but not particularly experienced off-piste for example.

If that sounds like you then get hold of some nice fat powder skis and practise with them, or take powder lessons/clinics to get over the novelty of skiing through the fine stuff.

Try another idea...

If it's backcountry skiing you're after, you don't have to cram into a chopper and act like a member of the special forces. Take a look at the Telemark technique for another means of getting away from the piste in IDEA 2, *Heroes of Telemark*.

Defining idea...

'*The sensual caress of waist deep cold smoke – glory in skiing virgin snow, in being the first to mark the powder with the signature of their run.*'
TIM CAHILL, one of the great modern writers of the great outdoors

How did it go?

Q   All I hear is heli ski – what about us snowboarders?

A   *Heli boarding is growing in popularity and most operations are happy to take boarders. Just make sure that you have a board suitable for powder (many operators rent powder skis but few rent boards). Collapsible ski poles are also popular amongst heli boarders.*

Q   Can I use an airbag avalanche safety system?

A   *Depends where you're going. Some Canadian operators aren't allowed to use them while heli skiing, and worldwide there are very few operators who provide avalanche airbags. Best to ask in advance.*

Q   Can I make jokes about 'Nam/death from above/having a big chopper'?

A   *Not really advisable, and in many places they aren't ever called 'choppers' but 'busses'.*

18
Taking the plunge

The long climb up to the highboard or the rocky outcrop. That stomach-turning moment of self-doubt just before the dive, the rush of air, the shock of water – then the elation and raging endorphin rush.

Diving is one of the oldest extreme sports known to man.

A dive from 26 m involves a three-second freefall and a maximum speed on hitting the water of 100 km/h. There is no body armour, no Kevlar, no crash helmet and no safety line. Just the you, the plunge and a skimpy bathing suit which may or may not still be in place as you surface. In 1998, Swiss diver and World High Diving Federation founder, Frederic Weill dived from a helicopter 26 m above Lake Verbano in Italy to publicise the WHDF and bring cliff diving to the world's attention (see below). It was an armstand forward double somersault pike with split, in case you were wondering. His trunks stayed on, in case you were wondering about that too. The highest dive on record is also attributed to a Swiss (well, they can't all be kept busy making cuckoo clocks) who performed a double back somersault from nearly 54 m up. Inexplicably there seems to be no reference to whether he emerged with or without Speedos.

Here's an idea for you...

A century ago trick diving emerged as a by-product of gymnasts who reduced their chances of injury by trying out new moves with water landings rather than risking a wipeout on the wooden floors then popular in gymnasiums. Divers can now return the favour by practicing their moves on trampolines to get used to the tucks, pikes and flips. As you try moves like summersaults get used to looking out for a point on the wall, such as a light or other feature, to spot as you turn over. A lot of diving coaches report that one of their biggest problems is stopping learner divers from shutting their eyes during the moves, and so reducing their own awareness of their mistakes.

Of course, you don't have to dive from 26 m or more to scare yourself witless, impress the opposite sex or risk losing your knickers. Standard diving highboards can be found at 5, 7.5 or 10 metres above the water.

Back in the 1800s diving was limited to a simple plunge into the wet stuff and the Brits usually performed the whole move with the arms held straight up in the air, a technique known as the English header. It is the Swedes who are credited with bringing in the swallow dive and, rather begrudgingly, the competitions began to accept that there was more to diving than simply trying to create a splash. Gymnasts from Sweden and Germany were in the habit of practising on beaches so that acrobatics could be tried out with the option of a softer landing. That developed into modern diving although for years separate competitions existed for 'plain' and 'fancy' diving.

Dives vary depending on whether they are forwards, backwards and in what direction they twist but there are still three basic body positions:

- the pike, in which the legs are straight and the body bends at the hips
- the tuck, in which the body bends at the hips and knees, drawing the thighs into the chest and keeping the heels into the bottom
- straight, where there is no bending at the joints although the back may arch.

If it's the fall that fascinates then maybe you should stay away from the highboard and instead take it to its logical limits with the bungee jump. See IDEA 22, *Boing – bungee jumping without tears.*

Try another idea...

When divers describe a 'free' diving position or move it means a combination of any of the above.

CLIFF DIVING

Everyone thinks of Acapulco when you mention cliff diving but the professional cliff divers tend to stay away from it because the landing area is shallow and the drop is not direct. In order to be sure of clearing the rocks on the way down, the Acapulco divers have to launch themselves several metres outwards which makes it nigh-on impossible to perform the kind of tricks that cliff divers look for.

Cliff diving is usually from a 25 m platform and landing is feet first, with three or four somersaults thrown in on the way down to keep the crowd amused. If you want to know more about the professional cliff diving circuit then take a look at www.procliffdivers.com.

'Those who can soar to the highest heights can also plunge to the deepest depths.'
L.M. MONTGOMERY, Canadian author – not that I remember any high-diving sequences in her *Anne of Green Gables*

Defining idea...

How did
it go? **Q   I'm fine turning summersaults on the trampoline but I don't feel
comfortable doing it off the diving board. Any ideas?**

A   *Certainly. A lot of people quite reasonably don't like to try tricks off the
board because of the fear of performing a bellyflop of mythic proportions.
One drill that's used to try and get the hang of straightening out from a
summersault is to crouch at the end of a lowboard, grabbing your shins and
tucking your chin down. That's where you'd end up if you'd just performed
a summersault. Now tip forward, rolling off the board (without bouncing)
and straighten up to enter the water cleanly. That should help you get used
to snapping into a good shape to enter cleanly.*

**Q   Aside from the occasional belly-busting misdive the thing that
kills me is headache and toothache. Does everyone suffer this?**

A   *No. Try a gumshield which will certainly stop you from crashing your teeth
together and may stop you gritting them before and during the dive (which
can lead to neck pain and headache).*

19

Big bore action

Bore surfing is right out there at the very extreme end of an already extreme sport.

Surfers often talk of taking on the big waves, measuring their height in tens of metres, but for these surfers it's the kilometres covered that are the mark of a true wild bore.

Tidal bores are a freak of nature whereby tides cause a wave that runs up river. The excitement comes when the wave hits at high tide into a river that has a progressively narrowing estuary to funnel and accelerate it. As such, bores are a rare phenomenon but there are between sixty and a hundred locations known around the world. Enthusiasts hunt them out because if you time a bore run right you could be riding that wave for miles instead of minutes. Timing is not as straightforward as you might hope. True, there are tide tables to help predict the bore, and there's plenty of historical data on better-known bores such as the Severn in the UK, but the number of factors involved (including wind strength, river level and others) means there is always an element of guesswork. Don't expect the bore

Here's an idea for you...

Before going out to kill yourself on the Quaintang why not try something eminently more sociable? The Dordogne is one of France's most tourist-friendly regions and at St Pardon there is a bore that moves at over 20 km/h. Come summer you can find up to a hundred would-be bore riders waiting for the wave here and those that catch it find themselves surfing alongside each other on a 400-metre-wide wave before meeting up for a glass of the local and a chance to admire the wave photos at the Café du Port.

to simply run straight up the river, either, since it may bounce off the banks like a massive wet pinball along the way.

The spiritual home of the sport is the river Severn in Gloucestershire, UK. The first recorded attempt to ride the 20 km/h Severn bore dates back to 21 July 1955, when Colonel James Churchill strode into the Severn with a surfboard under his arm. The colonel rode the bore for only a few hundred metres but in doing so a sport was born.

Since then a few dedicated bore riders have made certain bores their own. You can't now talk of the Severn bore without mentioning Steve King whose dedicated riding of the river culminated in a single unbroken surf run that carried him for ten kilometres over the course of an hour (try that in Hawaii). By far the easiest way to surf the Severn bore is on the net, thanks to the excellent BoreRiders site at www.boreriders.com. There are other major rideable bores around the world.

- Turnagain, Alaska. Turnagain is near Anchorage and thus, unsurprisingly, freezing. If that wasn't enough to put you off it also features quicksand and mudflats that the would-be bore surfer has to dodge. On the plus side it is the only bore in the world to offer midnight surfing and as such must surely feature on the 'to do' list of the real extreme surfer.

- Pororoca, Brazil. The mighty Amazon is the ultimate river and so it comes as no surprise that it hosts one of the ultimate bores – the Pororoca. Reported to travel as much as 200 km inland, the Pororoca is a celebrity even these days not least due to the cost of accessing the remote river sites in order to surf. Bore riders who have paddled out onto the Pororoca can also brag about the piranhas.

Every year there is a big wave competition organised at the Rio Araguari. The record is a ride lasting sixteen minutes and thirty-nine seconds.

- Shubenacadie, Canada. Before the Moncton Causeway shrank the Petitcodiac this was one of the largest bores in the world at over ten metres. However, in its reduced form it has been dubbed 'total bore' which is unfair because it can still reach three metres or so and has the unique distinction of occurring pretty much daily for which bore surfers continue to thank the heavens. More info from www.petitcodiac.org.

- The Quaintang Dragon, China. Said to create a roar that can be heard 30 km away and creating a wave 10 m high, the Quaintang Dragon is the fastest and most dangerous bore on the planet. An expedition to ride it in 1988 managed to stay atop the wave for only eleven seconds before it overcame one of the accompanying Zodiac rubber boats. Now there's a challenge for you, if you can wangle a permit from the Chinese government.

Try another idea...

If you're not quite ready for the big bore stuff just yet, then remind yourself of the basics in **IDEA 12, *Catching waves.***

Defining idea...

'*Nothing in the world is more flexible and yielding than water. Yet when it attacks the firm and the strong, none can withstand it, because they have no way to change it.*'
LAO TZU

Q **Can I have a go on a surf slipper or body board?**

A *Canoes of all sorts are common in the Dordogne and, yes, people do try on body boards but it is hard to get a decent ride on such a small platform.*

Q **Is a long board or a short board best for bore riding?**

A *Bores aren't really the place for trick moves – when you've been waiting all year for a particular wave you don't take the chance of losing it for the sake of an attempted aerial off the lip. Instead you want to catch it (not a given) and hold it, so the stability of the design means that most bore surfers go with long boards for the ride.*

20

Geronimo! – coasteering, kloofing and canyoning

Remember that moment in *Butch Cassidy and the Sundance Kid* when they find themselves teetering on the edge of a raging river canyon with a pursuing posse of gunmen at their backs?

Scale down the number of handguns on display, get real about the good looks of all involved and you've pretty much got the spirit of coasteering.

Let's just set the record straight. Lemmings do not, contrary to popular wisdom, commit suicide by hurling themselves off cliffs. Lemmings are too smart to do that sort of thing. It takes people to not only throw themselves off cliffs, but to pay others for the privilege of doing so.

Coasteering, as it's called in the UK, kloofing, as it's known in South Africa and canyoning, as it's called in the US, is the gentle art of continuing your mountainside or cliffside stroll even when the path runs out and the only way onwards is downwards. Even when 'downwards' would have the most feeble-minded lemming making an excuse and heading back to the car park.

Some kloofs/canyons are actually white-water rides where there is too little water to even float a kayak. Some tour companies take advantage of this by bringing body boards (small floating boards about the size of your torso) for a little impromptu white-water surfing along stretches of the route. Forewarned is forearmed so don't be afraid to ask questions before you go and if you're going to body surf through canyons ask if elbow protectors are a good idea. At the very least you may want to take some old fingerless gloves to save the skin on your palms.

Whichever name you call it or country you choose to try it in the opening act is the same. You will be kitted out with the appropriate gear, which usually means climbing helmets and quite possibly wetsuits. If you're coasteering in the UK then the chances are you're looking at the Welsh coast near St David's, in which case you will definitely be going in sheathed in a wetsuit from the neck down. Don't worry too much about the cold when coasteering/canyoning: I've tried it in Wales out of season and because you keep moving you won't notice it.

If you're being suited up in rubber then you may be given the option of wetsuit booties for your feet. If not, then you're never going to go far wrong with an old pair of trainers but make sure you're not so attached to them that you couldn't bring yourself to throw them away afterwards. You will be briefed on the route, including any climbs involved and – of course – where and when you will be expected to drop into the water below. Every route has its own specialities and it's worth asking beforehand whether the main appeal is the wildlife, the scenery, the adrenalin or various combinations of the lot. In some of the coastal routes there is a chance to encounter wildlife (such as seals and birds) that would normally be hidden from observers up on the cliffs; with river canyons it's the scenery that tends to take pride of place. You'll be guided, so there's no chance of getting lost, and with river canyons there's only one way to go in any case – downstream. That said, some canyons offer a lot more choice of variations along the same basic route and may allow you to invent your own jumps by climbing higher up the rock face before allowing gravity to take its course.

If it's the thought of out and out freefall that appeals then turn to bungee jumping at IDEA 22, _Boing_.

Try another idea...

Whatever you do never be tempted to dive in headfirst. Going in feet first may be a bad idea in polite society but in unknown water it's always the way to go. Don't forget that water varies around the world – in South Africa's Western Cape the natural tannins can make it look very dark brown and thus very deep even when in reality there's less than a metre between that twinkling surface and the rocks beneath. Don't jump into anything before checking that it has been jumped before. Of course the flip side of that is that pretty much every route has a section called 'suicide' kloof/jump/canyon. Don't get flustered by grand names: some such 'suicide' jumps wouldn't really give the jitters to a gerbil's grandma.

If you're worried about high jumps or white water then find out beforehand if there are different levels of course to choose from and whether they are no-way-back or not. In the UK coasteering routes are often graded: 'white' normally indicates white water, 'red' may require strong swimming skills. Because British routes are largely around the coast they may have a number of exit points along the route if it all gets a bit much. In the US and South Africa canyoning/kloofing routes tend to start at the top and make their way down so

Butch: 'All right. I'll jump first.'
Sundance: 'Nope.'
Butch: 'Then you jump first.'
Sundance: 'No, I said!'
Butch: 'What's the matter with you?!'
Sundance: (wildly embarrassed) 'I can't swim!'
From _Butch Cassidy and the Sundance Kid_

Defining idea...

remember that a single 'compulsory' jump means that there's no way back after that point. If you're unsure about jumps then ignore the peer pressure and find out if there's a route where jumps are optional. That way the whole party can have a ball without anxiety spoiling the day.

One last tip – go out and buy a disposable waterproof camera for each of you in the group. Don't be stingy and rely on just the one; get one for everyone. They cost very little and you will have a much better time if you are all trying to get the best embarrassing snaps of each other going bottom first into the foam.

How did it go?

Q   What do you mean I won't notice the cold? I get cold in the bath.

A   If you are prone to the shivers then a swimming cap or diver's hood is a small touch that makes a big difference (and you can take it off if you don't need it). Even a baseball cap will do in a pinch though you stand more chance of losing it after jumps.

Q   This is going to take all day isn't it? What about bodily functions?

A   If you're kloofing/canyoning then there will be plenty of bushes. If you're in the sea in a wetsuit then pee breaks mean getting over it and learning to central heat your suit the natural way. Food and water are usually provided, but if not take a small bag with sealed water bottles and food in Ziploc plastic bags. If you have to carry cash then remember to keep notes Ziploc'd and dry.

21

Tip top – sport climbing

Rock climbing is somewhere in between a three-dimensional chess game and an unusually slow choreographed dance. So-called 'sport' climbing makes that dance available to just about anyone.

That's not to say it is purely for beginners; sport climbing competitions can be as complex and demanding as you'd wish.

Sport climbing is the practice of climbing with pre-placed anchor points and often (but not necessarily) a top rope so that even the relative novice can learn the moves and mindset of climbing while reducing the risk of setting their own 'protections' when scaling the unknown. This just means that the focus is taken away from the intricacies of attaching yourself to the rock, and is more on the moves from one point to the next.

People have climbed for as long as they were bright enough to notice that some places were higher than others. No childhood is complete without at least one attempt to shin up a steep bank or hang off a tree, and rock climbing is a natural extension of that. If you've ever seen those vertigo-inducing pictures of climbers seemingly clinging like flies to sheer faces you'll know that it's an extension that

Here's an idea for you...

You don't have to be suspended hundreds of metres up to perfect your climbing moves. Practising traverses, grips and jams on rocks so low you don't need ropes for safety is called bouldering and has pretty much become a sport in its own right. Many indoor gyms even have a bouldering area where grips and overhangs are only a metre or so above thick landing mats. If you're bouldering outdoors (and for preference even when practicing indoors) then you should have a friend to act as a 'spotter' waiting to help catch you or slow your fall if you slip – even a tumble from a metre high can cause injury if you fall badly.

can go a very long way towards the extreme. Yet while the adrenaline factor of climbing is unquestioned it is also a surprisingly cerebral sport in which the techniques are really about problem solving in three dimensions.

The obvious place to get started in sport climbing is on an artificial climbing wall. These have popped up all over the placc and often take the form of fully-equipped indoor climbing gyms. Artificial climbing walls come complete with overhangs, cracks and hand or footholds as well as bolts you can hook onto with your carabiners (the D-shaped clips which all climbers carry). Usually the grips are colour coded or numbered to give different routes up the wall, so that while you can use absolutely any point that comes to hand (or foot) in the beginning you can progress by restricting yourself to prescribed routes of varying difficulty.

The first thing to learn when getting the hang of a climbing wall is a technique called 'belaying' which gives you the reassurance of a safety rope leading from you, up to a point above you which acts as a pulley, and then back down to a partner who can keep you safe even if you were to get it into your head to throw yourself backwards off the wall.

Climbing gyms will already have these top ropes suspended from points above the wall. To use them you will need to pull on a climbing harness which embraces your hips and thighs in a decidedly forward manner. You will then be shown how to tie on to the rope so it won't come undone while at the other end of the rope your belaying partner will be similarly harnessed up plus the addition of a belay device. The device works by adding enough friction to the rope so that your partner can easily apply a brake to your fall with one hand. As you climb up the rope the belayer takes in the slack, sliding it through the belay device in a precise sequence which ensures that the brake hand is always on the rope and in position ready to stop a fall. With the slack gone, even letting go of the wall altogether means the climber won't fall but will dangle instead. Not elegant, maybe, but infinitely less painful than plummeting.

Enjoying the slo-mo vertical choreography that is climbing? Then go a step further with tradding: see IDEA 35, *Rad tradding*.

Try another idea…

In order for this to work well it is essential to have a series of calls between climber and belayer that establish and check that each has tied on correctly and is aware of what the other is doing. Most climbing gyms will make you take a simple belay test to ensure you're ready to go play without supervision. And after that the wall is your oyster.

'A country can truly call itself sporting when the majority of its people feel a personal need for sport.'
PIERRE DE COUBERTIN, who set up the modern Olympic Games

Defining idea…

Q **My climbing partner weighs at least twice my body weight – even with a friction device I am afraid I will simply be hauled up into the air if he falls off the wall.**

A   *Simple – look around the floor of the gym and you will find bolts called bottom anchors, often with a short length of rope ready. Clip onto a bottom anchor and you will stay put even if your partner doesn't.*

Q **What's a GriGri? And why aren't I allowed to use one?**

A   *A GriGri is a great belaying device that works a bit like an automatic seat belt. If the belayer lets go with the brake hand and the rope starts to run, the GriGri will automatically snap shut on it and block any movement. Sounds foolproof but many climbing gyms work on the principle that you should first learn to use the simpler wire loop belay devices before you start to automate the process.*

22

Boing – bungee jumping without tears

Being tied to an oversized rubber band and shoved off something tall is one of the most truly sphincter-tightening sports our deranged imaginations have come up with to date.

Fortunately it is also one of the safest, and arguably one of the oldest, adventure sports known to humanity.

In pretty much any given action film involving heights the hero or heroine is pretty much guaranteed to be given the time-honoured advice of 'don't look down'. When you stand there at the top of a bungee jump and peer downwards you know exactly why they say that, and why it is as pointless a piece of advice as its close cousin 'don't panic'. You can't help but look down – whether or not you suffer from vertigo, we all have a fascination with the fear of falling. Look down just once and your stomach contracts to the size of a walnut. Every tube in your body goes into an agony of indecision about whether to lock down like a bear trap or open up and let fly. Look around and all you'll see is the hearty grins of those not about to jump. At which point someone will probably say something inane like 'ready?' and that's it, you're off: arms, legs and pretty much everything else akimbo.

Here's an idea for you...

Tired of traditional bungee, you globe-trotting daredevil, you? OK, then try reverse bungee. In reverse bungee you are strapped into a pod (usually two of you at once) which is suspended between two towers and connected to them both by enormous elastic bands. If you ever played with a catapult/slingshot when you were a kid then you can probably guess what comes next. The elastic takes up the slack, the pod is released and you go flying off into the sky. Most operators have a small video camera attached to the pod filming your reaction so when your stomach has returned to normal you can have a giggle at your zero-g gurning.

Bungee jumping goes way back. The first bungee jumpers most probably came from the small islands of Vanuatu in the South Pacific. The story varies slightly depending on who's doing the telling but the bottom line is that it became a rite of passage; young men on the threshold of manhood would hurl themselves off towers with springy vines tied around their ankles. You've got to admit that as an introduction to adult life the rush of bowel-loosening blind panic is a pretty accurate picture of the way things are going to go. Although that could just be my life.

Whatever, the young David Attenborough took a BBC film crew down to Vanuatu and came back with film of the 'land divers' of Pentecost Island. This promptly inspired the members of the Oxford University Dangerous Sports Club to use elastic ropes – bungees – to tie themselves to the Clifton Suspension Bridge prior to throwing themselves off. They chose 1 April 1979 for their jump but the April Fool joke was really on the rest of us as the idea of commercial bungee was born.

It took a New Zealander called A.J. Hackett to popularise it in the 80s, and in a neat bit of self-promotion he took a dive off the Eiffel tower in 1987 and created himself a thriving business in the process. Now bungee jumping can be found all over the world, from bridges, towers and even cranes in car parks. New Zealand remains the Mecca of bungee with a wide range of sites, but a tour of the world's best places would probably include:

- Bloukrans Bridge, South Africa: the world's highest commercial jump at 216 m.
- Viaduc de la Souleuvre, France: beautiful scenic viaduct site run by A.J. Hackett in Normandy.
- Victoria Falls, Zimbabwe: take a plunge against the backdrop of the 'smoke that thunders'.
- Queenstown, New Zealand: the 'capital' of the bungee world.

Or of course you could just jump off a crane in a car park; the choice is yours.

Variations on the classic swan dive jump include the bat where you start off head down, held by your ankles; the lovers' leap where you jump in tandem with another person (not necessarily your lover) and the water splash where you briefly touch the water at the bottom of the jump. Some sites allow you to take a running

If bungee is to your taste then why not take it one step further and do it without the rope? Stupid idea? Maybe, but that's what IDEA 41, *Scare yourself witless with SCAD*, is all about.

Try another idea...

'One small step for man; one giant leap for mankind.'
NEIL ARMSTRONG, astronaut, readying himself for a running-start jump

Defining idea...

jump off the top, others (such as A.J. Hackett's in France) insist that you have done a minimum number of standard jumps before you start experimenting with the fancy stuff. Where it's on offer, a jump at night is another way of turning up the adrenaline dial. For the ultimate in bungee you could always look out for operators that offer heli bungee. All the fear of falling plus the roar of rotors and the force of the downdraft.

How did it go?

Q I've done lots of normal bungee jumps but the site nearest me doesn't offer any 'trick' jumps like running starts or the bat. Any ideas on how to spice up my jump life?

A *Sure. If you want a simple trick to make the whole thing a bit more exciting then just turn round and drop backwards at the start, instead of swan diving.*

Q Isn't it dangerous?

A *Don't tell anyone but the answer is no. Professional operators adhere to strict rules about breaking strains and stretch dynamics so bungee is probably the safest 'dangerous' sport there is. Obviously all bets are off if you try and create your own bungee by tying rubber bands together and jumping off the banisters.*

23

Messing about in boats

Whether you are looking for serene sailing or want to hang off the edge of the boat on a trapeze, dinghies can provide the precise level of adventure for anyone at any age.

Wherever there is a puddle deep enough to float a boat in you can be sure to find someone trying to rig a dinghy and sail.

Sailing somehow manages to be many sports in one, which is perhaps why it has such broad appeal. On a calm sunny day it is as serene and elegant a sport as you could wish for, if lying back and watching the cat's paws of wind toying with a sail can honestly be called a sport. At the other extreme a racing dinghy, heeled hard over and scudding through the spray with you hanging off it hooked up to a trapeze, can be every bit as white knuckle as white-water sports.

Dinghies come in all shapes and sizes from Lasers and other racers that look more like windsurfing boards than boats to the reassuringly wide-bottomed and matronly wooden Wayfarers. Many beach resorts also now offer one-man catamarans for first-timers and learners. The more stable (and lower performance) boats are more

Here's an idea for you... **Try sailing without using a rudder. You'll notice very quickly that sail trim and the angle of heel will affect the boat's handling but you may not have realised that you can harness these forces to steer. Choose a quiet patch of water in conditions of mild wind; centre and secure the tiller with a bungee cord so you don't lose it in case of capsize. Now try to sail a course just using sail trim to steer. You'll be surprised to find that you can sail quite happily without a rudder and in the process you will hone your boat handling to a fine art.**

reassuring for beginners but in general whatever type of dinghy you choose it is a very easy sport to get going on.

Most introductory courses start with a brief introduction to the parts of the boat, the rigging and a few basic nautical terms before launching into the control of sail and steering by means of the tiller and the sheets (the ropes that control sails). After that you're off, learning to turn with the wind behind you (gybe) or to zigzag across the face of it (tack) so that you can complete a triangular course.

We don't (yet) have compulsory licences for sailing so it's up to you how much or little tuition you want to take though I would strongly recommend the Royal Yachting Association (RYA) dinghy sailing course in the UK and its equivalents worldwide for the mix of a little theory and a lot of practical application. A couple of weekends – or three or four days on the beach – is all you need to come away with a little certification and a big dollop of confidence.

Sailing takes no time to learn and years to master, so you can be up and running in an hour or so and sailing happily for the rest of your life. You may be content to simply noodle around in circles, reliving children's stories from your youth, or you may want to speed things up a bit by starting to race. Racing is commonly seen as the best way of learning in a hurry. It takes a bit of commonsense so as not to get in the way of others, but most clubs are more than happy to encourage beginners to have a go. There is no quicker way of gaining boat-handling skills and recognising those fine touches that distinguish the master mariners from those merely messing about (perfectly noble ambition though that is).

> If being on the water is what you want, but without the hassle of learning to sail, then take a look at IDEA 44, Sea kayaking.
>
> *Try another idea...*

Never let anyone try to convince you that dinghy sailing isn't real sailing, or is somehow inferior to racing in forty-metre monsters. For many purists dinghy sailing is the only real deal due to the way that even the slightest detail of your boat handling will affect the craft's performance. It offers an understanding of wave and water and requires a delicacy of touch that can sometimes be lacking in larger boats. A love of dinghies has inspired people to perform all manner of extreme feats and epic journeys in craft little larger than a bathtub.

> 'Nice? It's the ONLY thing' said the Water Rat solemnly, as he leant forward for his stroke. 'Believe me, my young friend, there is NOTHING – absolutely nothing – half so much worth doing as simply messing about in boats.'
> KENNETH GRAHAME, *The Wind in the Willows*
>
> *Defining idea...*

Q **When I try to gybe I often find that the boat just doesn't want to, which means we don't. Why?**

A *Gybing is actually no harder than tacking, it's just that with the wind full behind the sail the forces involved may be a bit greater. To control the sail and bring it round you'll need to sheet it in as hard as you possibly can before turning the tiller and crying 'gybe-oh'. Think of sheeting in as a way of keeping a tight leash on the beastie.*

Q **I've tried taking a course but still find myself unsure – is there any other way of learning the ropes?**

A *Certainly; the most traditional way of learning more about boats large or small is to offer to crew on someone else's boat. Make it very clear what level of expertise you have so that nobody expects more of you than you can deliver, and remember to take the time to a) look around and learn from others and b) enjoy yourself.*

24

Tour de force

Cycle touring is fast shaking off its image as the holiday of choice for stamp collectors...

Tours are now on offer to pretty much every corner of the globe and in packages as easy or as demanding as you could wish for.

Want to wobble slowly through the wine regions of France from gîte to gîte while your luggage is driven on ahead to wait for your arrival? Perhaps your idea of cycling is to freewheel the Karakorum highway or pedal your way across Patagonia. Cycling can be for softies or fitness fanatics, and at a reasonable touring rate – anywhere from 50 (very easy) to 100 km a day – you can cover a surprising amount of ground.

Everyone knows how to cycle, of course – you famously never forget – but if you're not a regular cyclist you should prepare yourself carefully before plunging into a week's solid peddling. First off, you should think about the fitness levels of everyone in the group – you can only go as fast as the slowest, after all. Next, you have to consider if you are going to take your own gear or sign up with a tour that transports your luggage by car to your destination every day. If you are, then is it just you and your loved ones or will you be joined by strangers? How are you going

OK, no beating around the bush, so to speak. One of the big problems for both sexes when embarking on a bike tour is pain in the nether regions. Agony here can ruin a holiday so why not take some steps to soothe the soreness? First check your saddle – is it pointed slightly upwards? That'll be the culprit. Secondly, try standing regularly on the pedals to help blood flow. Thirdly, go buy a gel saddle cover to make the ride more comfy. If that doesn't do it then invest in an 'anatomical' saddle which has a hole in the crucial spot to take the pressure off. Vaseline and other anti-chafing gels are great for rough skin but if it turns out to be a rash then head for the chemist rather than grimly pedalling through a daily serving of petroleum jelly and moist gusset.

to cope if you find you loathe the strangers with a passion previously only reserved for estate agents and cold-calling telesales staff?

If you're going with the independent approach then make sure that you can fit everything into your panniers and, having done so, that you can still haul your bike up and down a step or two. You don't want find out how much it all weighs for the first time when you're in a hurry offloading a pannier-laden bike from one train, prior to loading it onto another.

If you're thinking of cycle touring then here's a piece of excellent advice: 'Bicycle made for two'? Just say no. Tandems may be a giggle and make perfect sense when you're experienced with them but you will be surprised how hard they are to get started on. You have to balance and counterbalance each other as you both pedal as one and wobble your way up to speed. Of course, once moving everything is hunky-dory but until you have momentum on your side you are as stylish as a drunk on a unicycle.

Having safely left the tandem in the garage here are a few things I would recommend taking:

If you love bikes but don't do roads then try IDEA 26, Mountain biking.

Try another idea...

- Two pairs of cycling shorts and tops so that if you can't wash your kit that evening, you have a clean outfit the next day (infections are less than pretty). Invest in modern 'wicking' fabric sportswear as it is lightweight and dries fast after washing (lurid colours optional).
- Evening wear such as a spare T-shirt and light trousers.
- A fleece and a waterproof, breathable jacket.
- A helmet.
- Water bottles – plenty of them; and sterilising tablets to keep them free from bugs in the heat.
- Loads of Ziploc plastic bags in various sizes to keep everything dry.
- Lightweight GPS.
- Spare pair of legs.
- Repair kit, spare inner tube, tyre levers and a pump (rehearse changing your inner tube so you don't have to try and remember how to do it while stuck in the rain by a foreign highway).

Don't take on distances you're not used to, do have a backup plan in case it all goes pear-shaped (hint, trains are a great backup plan, planes aren't). Do remember to ensure that everyone else is fit enough – that includes kids and toddlers who may turn out to suffer motion sickness. Don't feel obliged to shave your legs or wear Lycra festooned with the logo of Spanish telecoms operators or Swiss watch manufacturers but, on the other hand, if that's what makes you happy then allez allez. More power to your straining thighs.

'Every time I see an adult on a bicycle, I no longer despair for the future of the human race.'
H.G. WELLS

Defining idea...

101

How did it go?

Q **I must have done something rotten to the Inner Tube Fairy when I was a kid – I get punctures every day. Do you know how much fun that isn't?**

A *Oh I do, I do. Try armoured tyres that will shake off most roadside broken glass, etc. 'Gatorskins' and 'Armadillos' are popular examples.*

Q **Any tips for dealing with chasing dogs?**

A *Pedal harder? Seriously, try pulling out one of your water bottles and squirting it at the dog's face – it usually stops them for long enough for you to get away.*

25

The big blue

Some people have always wanted to fly like birds, others have dreamed of delving the depths like loose-limbed dolphins. For them freediving is the purest experience of the water.

It's the closest you can get to being a fish.

From the day you first duck-dived under the water you probably began to wonder just how long you could stay down. Freediving in all its forms is an exploration of that curiosity – how deep, or for how long, can people go underwater? For some it has a slightly spiritual element, not least since the best breath holders often turn to techniques from oriental religions in the quest for greater control over lungs and heart. Of course, films (remember *The Big Blue*?) TV ads and pictures in glossy magazines all serve to play up its glamour, with lean-limbed dive gods of both sexes looking fetching in their ultra-tight suits as they follow a slim white line into the deepest of deep blues.

It might come as a surprise, then, to find that not all freediving involves the sea. Freediving, also known as breath-hold diving, skin-diving and apnea, is a general term for at least seven different disciplines. Although films and media have tended to focus on the record-breaking deep dives some disciplines don't involve depths and can be practised in the swimming pool. In terms of competition there are three main areas: constant ballast, static apnea and dynamic apnea.

Here's an idea for you...

Freedive sports don't just have to mean deeper or longer. Get in touch with your local swimming pool or diving club and ask about Octopush – underwater hockey. Played in a swimming pool, it uses a puck that slides along the bottom and stumpy one-handed 'sticks' that are used to push the puck at the goals. The catch, of course, is that you can only stay in control at the bottom for as long as you can hold your breath. The no-limits approach of apneists in general means that some Austrians have even experimented with underwater ice hockey – the puck is buoyant and skims along under the surface of the ice. Don't believe it? Check the video at www.apneaplanet.com.

Constant ballast is a strange name but what it means is that you come up with what you go down with – mainly yourself. The swimmer (apneist, as some insist) dives and ascends using only their own strength, touching the cable only once at the bottom of the dive when it's time to start ascending. Many competitions have tags set at different depths and the diver only touches the cable to pluck the deepest tag they can reach before surfacing. Just to add to the fun constant ballast comes in both finless and finny disciplines – so with or without the frogfeet.

Static apnea means you hold your breath for as long as you can, either underwater or just with your face under the surface. It's not as glam as the glossy pictures of blue water but if you tire of the exotic locations, fabulous scenery and long-limbed entourages you could always have a go at static apnea in a large soup bowl if you had a mind to. Getting sponsorship might be a touch tricky, though.

Dynamic apnea is what you started to do at school when you swore you could swim a width underwater. Competitors are marked on how far they swim under the surface. It too comes in finned and finless variations.

The stuff that gets the most media attention, however is variable ballast, and the gloriously named no limits class. Variable ballast means you don't have to bring up that which took you down and so you can descend using a weighted 'sled' of a fixed maximum weight (35 kg) before coming up under your own steam (and, yes, you can pull on the cable). No limits means pretty much that and translates to brain-bending depths achieved by descending on a weighted sled (no limit to the weight, naturally) and coming back by firing up a gas-inflated balloon – the underwater equivalent of an ejector seat. Depth records are constantly being broken but with constant ballast having reached the 100 m mark, and no limits going beyond 170 m (by comparison most scuba dives are limited to a maximum depth of about 40 m) the argument rages over just where the limit lies.

In all apnea disciplines you fail the dive if you black out – a very common problem due to an interesting freak of physiology called shallow-water hypoxia which tends to strike just as you surface. The dangers of blackouts and pressure injury (for the deep divers) cannot be overestimated, and every year athletes are lost to the water, so the importance of training and supervision can't be overestimated either. If you're interested in giving it a whirl then the best place to start is in a diver training tank (often 30 m deep). To learn more about freediving where you live you only need to search Google for 'freediving lessons' or try websites like www.extremesportscafe.com to find out more.

Fancy exploring the deep blue while still hearing the reassuring sound of your own breathing? Then take a look at IDEA 47, *Simply scuba*.

Try another idea...

'Ah! Sir, live – live in the bosom of the waters! There only is independence! There I recognise no masters! There I am free!'
CAPTAIN NEMO, in *20,000 Leagues under the Sea* by Jules Verne

Defining idea...

Q **I only have to hold my breath for a minute and the urge to breathe becomes unbearable – how can freediving be possible?**

A *Initially you think that the first signs of needing to breathe mean the end of your dive, but after a while you learn to overcome that and extend the abilities of your body.*

Q **I hear that taking really heaving breaths in and out will extend my dives, is this true?**

A *Yes, hyperventilation before you dive flushes out more carbon dioxide from your lungs and it's the build up of carbon dioxide, rather than the shortage of oxygen, that triggers breathing. It's a first step but not as effective as learning to calm yourself down and lower your pulse which greatly extends your capacity underwater.*

Q **Great, so I can try hyperventilating and static apnea in the bath, then?**

A *Not a good idea. Unsupervised apnea is a recipe for disaster, even in the seemingly safe confines of a bathroom. If you want to learn, do so under proper supervision.*

26

Mountain biking

You never forget how to ride a bike, right? Try telling yourself that through your gritted teeth as you white-knuckle it down a gravelly hill face while trying to bunny-hop the fallen trees.

Real off-roading is a total blast.

Most mountain bikes, a bit like most 4x4s actually, never have to tackle anything more risky than the route to the local shops, which is a shame. Modern off-road bikes are near indestructible and have a surprising ability to ride right over the rough stuff and stay upright – given half a chance. Of course, you don't have to hit the hairy high ground to have fun on a mountain bike, and you may simply want to take it for a gentle mooch through the scenery, but chances are that sooner or later you are going to find yourself going slightly faster than you meant to over terrain that seems to have been designed by whoever did the lunar craters. And that's when the fun begins.

Downhilling on a road bike is called freewheeling, and has associations of effortlessness and smoothness. Downhilling on a mountain bike is usually called 'oh my god' and seems to involve a lot of grimacing punctuated by the occasional crash. Here are a few tips for minimising the latter.

Here's an idea for you...

Most of us cycle so far within the bounds of safety that we haven't even locked up the back wheel in a skid since the first and only time it happened to us as kids. So try getting used to the feeling of controlling the uncontrolled with your own skid pan. Find yourself a safe piece of open ground (if you're using a car park make sure you're as far as possible from gleaming, expensive-looking motors) and drop a sheet of ply or cardboard on the ground. Cycle at it full tilt and as your back wheel goes over it slam the back brake on full. The back wheel should lock and take the board with it, so you now power slide. It's a great way of getting used to steering in the slides.

■ If you're using a hired bike then check the seat height (it should be at about hip-height as you stand next to the bike) before you get on. Try the brakes right away – not going into that corner with a car coming the other way.

■ Get used to standing on the pedals with both feet at the same height, particularly as you throw yourself into the twisty stuff. Personal experience dictates that if you have one pedal lower than the other it will catch on a rock and pitch you off the bike faster than a bucking horse. Resist the temptation to lock out your knees and instead keep them slightly soft and bent – all the better to absorb the jolts and judders and protect them.

■ Be aware of your weight and the way it affects your centre of gravity. Shifting your weight forward over the bike helps keep the front wheel in contact with the ground. That's essential for tough uphilling and may make all the difference between keeping and losing control when steering on rough ground. If you are going to reach for the front brake (often not the best idea) then shift your weight backwards first to try and avoid the bike dumping you off the front like a bucking bronco.

- Believe in the bike. It's almost certainly capable of handling much hairier terrain than you are, so instead of getting scared at the first bumps and potholes try to relax and go with the flow. Yes, you are going to skid. Yes, you are going to bounce across the track like a drunk playing hopscotch on the deck of a trawler. Enjoy it and focus on balance, not brakes.

- It may seem counterintuitive at first but a bit of speed will help your stability, so don't be afraid to give it a bit of welly as you come up to the bumpy bits.

- Take it easy on the brakes and try to 'feather' them rather than grabbing a fistful of levers. Slamming on the anchors is one of the fastest ways of getting intimate with the ground and your best chance of staying upright and unbloodied is to give the brakes a break and instead focus on steering around/over/through obstacles. Oh, and grimly hanging on in there for dear life, of course.

- Don't forget the plasters and antiseptic.

Try another idea...

If you really fancy the off-road stuff then why not combine it with running and swimming and give Xterra cross-country triathlon a go? Take a peek at **IDEA 51**, *Xterra Xcitement*, for more.

Defini idea...

'*Life is like riding a bicycle. To keep your balance you must keep moving.*'
ALBERT EINSTEIN, a man who knew to stay off the brakes

111

Q **I've tried the skid-pan idea and only skidded for a second or so, what am I doing wrong?**

A *A couple of possibles – you might be unintentionally touching the front brake at the same time, or your board may be a bit big so that your front wheel is still on it as you slam on the back brakes.*

Q **I keep missing the board, other than practise over and over what can I do?**

A *You're not doing this on your own, are you? Unless you're a total sad no-mates you should be able to drum up another one or two similarly deranged characters and practise together. Then as you go hell for leather at the board just have one of them watch your wheels and shout 'now'. That way there's also someone there to laugh their head off and pick you off the tarmac when you get it wrong.*

27

Trekking

Journeying by foot across the world's wild places is almost irresistible for anyone who has ever watched a natural history programme on TV.

You can go further than you ever dreamed — just be sure you're prepared for what you find when you get there.

Ten years ago people who liked the outdoors went 'hiking'. For reasons as yet unknown to fashion, this involved knee socks, stout walking sticks, unspeakably painful boots and lashings of tartan. Now the adventure sport revolution means that the kind of people who would once have thought twice before embarking on a stroll in the UK's Lake District are rocking up to tour operators and demanding trips to Everest base camp or volcano summits in Guatemala. And quite right too. In the process trekking has become definitely cool; tartan has been ousted by Gore-tex, and where once only explorers and gap-year students could be found at the peak of Mount Kenya you are now just as likely to bump into that nice little old lady from the local shop.

Of course there is a down side to this. There is a kind of Adventure Arms Race whereby if Dave down the road made it to K2 Base Camp, then John will look like a big softie unless he tromps up the Trango Tower. Hand in hand with that is the

Here's an idea for you...

Take a decent pair of collapsible trekking poles with you – the most popular are made by Leki and are made of aluminium, weigh next to nothing and can be adjusted to the right height simply by twisting them. Trekking poles give you greater stability and, most importantly, take the weight off your legs and back by bringing the upper body into the equation. They increase comfort, endurance and make for excellent sword fights when you're celebrating having bagged that summit.

familiarity-breeds-contempt factor whereby destinations that were once reserved for hardcore explorers are now seen as simple holiday jaunts. I once met two blokes who saw no problem in yomping up Kilimanjaro dressed in T-shirts and shorts. They were happily complacent since lots of people had trekked up the mountain, and besides it was in Africa and therefore hot. Even the mention of the permanent glacier at the summit didn't make them think about the need for planning. 'It's called the Coca-Cola route,' one of them pointed out, 'how hard can it be?' As it happens, it was hard enough to take the lives of three people over the course of the next five days but fortunately our friends in the skimpy trousers made it through with nothing more serious than frozen knees and red faces. Just because others have done it doesn't take away the need for, or benefits of, extensive preparation.

Trekking tours are available the world over, from steppes to savannah, rock faces to rainforest, and are tailored to suit every ability, age group and degree of hardiness. My recommendation is undoubtedly to get out there and go for it, but be aware that there are certain factors that will not feature in even the most conscientious operator's descriptions.

Leaving out all the obvious stuff about your degree of physical fitness (just be honest with yourself) or the importance of jabs (take proper advice and remember to see it through – including finishing all courses of pills), the single greatest problem people have is that 'trekking' so often seems to mean 'uphill'. Nobody can really prepare you for altitude sickness because it varies so much from one person to the next. Fit people seem as likely to suffer as the unfit, and despite being told many times that fatties were more likely to suffer than thinnies personal experience suggests that it is pretty much totally random. So let's just imagine that once you're over 3000 m you're going to get chipolata fingers, random headaches and occasional nausea. Green tea may help, but by far the best way to counter altitude sickness is to take the time to acclimatise. Which means taking your time to go up and taking as many rest days as your body dictates. Unfortunately that is often at odds with the scheduling of tour operators and so rather than asking why a trek is so cheap, make sure that you ask how much time you will have to acclimatise on the way up. It would be a shame to make it to the summit only to have your view spoilt by a blinding headache and the overpowering urge to unleash last night's supper. The top of Kilimanjaro, the base camps of Everest and K2, and indeed high places the world over, are littered with people who spent a fortune on fancy shoes, saved a few shillings on the tour – and would now give their life savings to be back at sea level.

If you love the great outdoors, enjoy physical effort, but find walking a little plodding you could always try the high speed walking holidays known as ultrarunning – see IDEA 52, *Going ultra*.

Try another idea…

'During one of my treks through Afghanistan, we lost our corkscrew. We were compelled to live on food and water for several days.'
W.C. FIELDS

Defining idea…

115

How did it go?

Q How much stuff will I have to carry?

A   *If you're hiring porters (which will be appreciated by the local economy) then you will have to carry little other than your food, water and waterproofs for the day. Remember that wherever you go you will be limited by the availability of water along the way since even porters won't be able to carry enough water for you all for more than a couple of days.*

Q Any recommendations for bedding?

A   *Get advice from local experts on the right thickness of sleeping bag and give a thought to packing a Thermorest or similar inflatable mattress. They're light, pack small and because they trap a layer of air between you and the cold, hard ground, they provide great insulation. Good sleep makes all the difference between grinning and gritting it out.*

28

Catching air

Kite surfing (sometimes called kiteboarding) is an inspired combination of elements of wakeboarding, windsurfing, surfing and paragliding all brought together in one fast, furious, low-level flight through the wave crests.

It doesn't sound like it should be so hard. But the sheer power of a full-size kite flying in a strong wind is like nothing you've ever felt on a windsurf board.

We all flew kites when we were kids… and if you've managed to stand up on a surf or windsurf board then kite surfing should just be a question of putting the two together, no? If you've already tried kite surfing you're probably smirking right now. A power kite is about five square metres in size, can be flown in wind that would have windsurfers safely tucked up in a bar, and is strong enough to pluck you and your board from the sea and whisk you through the air before dropping you back down. With a bit of work this may even happen because you want it to.

Learning all this is a matter of days, not hours. In the words of the British Kite Surfing Association: 'typically it takes at least three days just learning to get up on the board once you have mastered the kite flying and body dragging, which will take most people new to it at least another three to five days.' Those of us who have

Here's an idea for you...

Whether you're learning the ropes for the first time or fine-tuning your skills for breathtaking air launches, then practice makes perfect. No problem if you happen to own a beachfront condo; for the rest of us, however, the big blue is something we only get to play with on holidays. So practise on land. Combine a skateboard or snakeboard with a kite and you can have fun tearing up the tarmac or blasting down the byways while learning skills that can be directly applied to your surfing. The board of choice, however, for land-based kiteboarding is a mountain board – off-road boards that look like the result of a night of passion between a skateboard and a Landrover.

difficulty chewing gum and walking at the same time can add a few more days to that estimate.

The good news is that you can break it all down into the component skills and master each of those before attempting to bring them all together. For beginners the best way of starting is safely back on terra firma. Standing around in a field flying a big kite may not be everyone's idea of an adventure sport but it's a lot easier to learn there than while balancing on a plastic plank with the ocean trying to yank your legs out from underneath you. A lot of schools recommend that you start by flying smaller kites, then move up to the big boys. That's sound advice, but remember that as well as size there is another key difference between the types of kite. Once upon a time all surf kites were two line, meaning you only had two control lines to worry about at once. Now a lot of surfers/flyers prefer the degree of control offered by four lines, so if you are going to end up quad line surfing then it makes sense to practice with the right number of bits of string right from the start.

Even when you've mastered flying a full-size power kite it's not yet time to put that together with the board. The next step is body surfing, where you get used to launching the kite in the water and using it to control where it takes you. Body surfing is the nice name for this, body dragging is more accurate.

Fancy harnessing the wind and skimming the wave crests but not sure about kite surf kit being available where you're going? Then maybe this will float your boat – try IDEA 45, Windsurfing.

Try another idea...

Board skills are the last part of the equation and here there's no doubt that surfing or windsurfing experience is going to stand you in good stead. If you've never boarded at all beforehand, then don't be surprised if the school starts you off on dry land with a board set on a pivot. It may look like the boarding equivalent of air guitar but there are distinct advantages to picking up the basics on dry land. That's coming from someone who made their boarding debut by spending an entire day falling off a windsurfer into a freezing lake. If you're ready to board, you've got your head around the control lines and you've played at being a menace to shipping while body dragging, then it's time to point yourself at the waves and grab air. And fall off, naturally.

Which is a great moment to mention that some kites are designed to be relaunched from the water – ask your friendly kite surf vendor to show you which ones.

'He who would learn to fly one day must first learn to stand and walk and run and climb and dance; one cannot fly into flying.'
FRIEDRICH NIETZSCHE

Defining idea...

How did it go?

Q I've been boarding (surf and wind) pretty much since I was old enough to swim and kite surfing is coming naturally. I'm grabbing air at will – so where would I look to make it that little bit wilder?

A *Time to follow the surfers. Kite surfers have been launching off waves for some time in the search for more airtime but the argument still rages about what a good kite surfer can do when faced with serious walls of water. Just be very sure that you're not going to pose a menace to traditional surfers if you join them on their favourite spots.*

Q I live a largely landlocked existence so I'm keen to practice on dry land – you mention mountain boards but is there really any advantage over the old skateboard in my attic?

A *There is indeed. The mountain boards have much larger wheels, greater ground clearance and trucks that are built with off-road in mind. Which means that even in the average car park you're less likely to find that you and the kite are going one way while the board has come to rest in the gutter.*

29

Paddle your own canoe

Canoes, or river kayaks, are all things to all paddlers. They can be transport, a fast track to fitness, race machines – or platforms for photography, fishing or family outings.

All you need to do is choose your canoe according to your needs... and paddle it.

There's more to river canoeing than just pointing downstream and going with the flow. Though, frankly, if that was all there was it would still be a very fine way of whiling away the days. Canoeing, whether in open 'Indian' canoes or decked-over kayaks, is gloriously easy to begin, and opens up a world of opportunities when you're out on the water.

The first step to true autonomy on the river is understanding that you are not condemned to drift downstream forever like mere lumber. Nor do you have to be some kind of adrenalin junky, battling holes and eddies to stay upright. In between the two there are vast tracts of river just waiting to be your playground as long as you learn how to play.

Here's an idea for you...

The benefits of the Eskimo roll are obvious; the problem is that it can seem daunting to learn. So break it down. Start in a nice warm swimming pool and line up with the edge. Put your hands on the side of the pool and get used to the feeling of tipping over as far as you can, then righting yourself with a hip flick. Your hands will save you from going right over. When you've got the hip roll try to add the paddle stroke but do so in the shallow end with a mate holding the end of the canoe, ready to give a bit of help flipping you if you don't look like making it. That way you'll have more time practising rolling and less swimming out and getting back into the kayak.

Indian canoes often look less daunting to the newcomer because they are open and the paddle has just the one blade. Certainly they are easier to get in and out of and can often carry more equipment, but make sure it's well stowed in case of capsize. Kayaks are limited to one or two people, and look uncomfortable with their bolt-upright sitting position and closeness to the water. That's more than compensated for, however, by their manoeuvrability and rough-water handling. If you're going for a two person, by the way, then it's normal practice to put the person with the most experience in the stern (back) since that's the position it's easiest to steer from.

Properly kitted up, with a flotation vest and a helmet, playtime should start off with a few of the basics.

■ Getting in and out – no kidding, you'd be surprised how many people have never heard of the rule about standing up in a boat. When that boat is less than a metre wide the results are predictable.

- Getting out when the boat has tipped over. Sooner or later you'll find yourself unwittingly in, rather than on, the watery world. Keeping your calm, detaching your spray deck (if you are using one) and swimming out and up is all about keeping your head.

If you're looking for relaxed, long-distance canoeing – you'll want to read about IDEA 44, *Sea kayaking*. Prefer the frantic, frenzied, adrenalin-fuelled version of the sport? Then turn to IDEA 42, *Wild-water and white-water slalom*.

Try another idea...

- Forward, backward, and turning strokes (sweeps).

- Bracing. Because it's soooo much more fun if you don't have to keep swimming out and righting an overturned canoe. Brace strokes are the paddling equivalent of putting an arm out to stop yourself falling over. They come in various flavours (such as high brace or low brace) depending on the arm positions, which are themselves often dictated by what you were doing at the time the boat started to tip. Mastering the brace means you can hold a canoe in position even when heeled right over and seemingly about to capsize.

- Eskimo rolls. An Eskimo roll, even a really clumsy Eskimo roll, is a thing of beauty – not least for the rollee, for whom it means the difference between being upside down and underwater and rightways up and merely waterlogged. If you take tuition (and you won't regret it if you do) you may be surprised to find that rolling is often seen as an optional rather than an essential technique. This is fair enough – people often balk at the idea of deliberately capsizing then relying on a new

'Originality is unexplored territory. You get there by carrying a canoe; you can't take a taxi.'
ALAN ALDA

Defining idea...

123

technique to get them back to the surface and air, sweet air. Short term, a mastery of the brace and the ability to swim will see you through. In the long term, however, you'll never meet a keen kayaker who doesn't boast at least a basic roll, and most have a repertoire of variations, not least since – psychologically – the ability to right a boat instantly and unaided is one of the key moments of mastery.

■ Eddy practice. Get used to going into and out of eddies flowing downstream of rocks.

■ Current practice. Get used to crossing rivers, as well as going up and downstream. Notice that currents don't simply run parallel to the bank but instead trace their own logic across the waterways.

How did it go?

Q   Kayaking is great. Getting in and out of the water is still a tippy nightmare. Can you help?

A   *Try using your paddle more as a stabilizer, much like an outrigger with the blade flat on the water. You can rest your paddle on the river bank for support, or against the bottom in shallow water. Remember to ease in and out with no sudden movements.*

Q   I'm a strong person and have a nice, clean, straight stroke, yet I don't seem to have the power of some of my peers. Any idea why?

A   *Sounds daft but are you using your legs? Kayak racers recommend 'cycling' – bracing with the opposite leg to the side you are paddling on to get extra tension and force behind the stroke.*

30
Triple fun – triathlon

Triathlon is a very recent sport, having only surfaced in the 70s, but it has spread far and wide as people have been seduced by the particular pleasures of multi-sport.

While long distance running is exhausting and hard on your joints, triathlon's mix and match approach means that even an event lasting hours leaves you remarkably fresh and ready for more.

A lot of people are put off by a worry that a multi-discipline event will prove complex but in practice anyone can get into triathlon – even if you run like a duck, cycle like a fish and swim like a bicycle. Some people get into a three-discipline event just because they can. If you're already a good swimmer, cyclist and runner, then why not? Others, however, like myself, ended up doing triathlon because they weren't.

My route to triathlon started when I was advised to take up swimming to ease some particularly gnarly back trouble. The only catch was that I swam like a brick. I took some adult lessons and got better, but realised that I needed more help to progress as I wasn't going to do it on my own. There was no way I could join a swimming club as they would all be swimmers and would laugh at me, but a *triathlon* club,

Here's an idea for you...

While the sprint distance is often referred to as the shortest triathlon there are smaller ones organised just as tasters. Often called a 'Try a Tri' or a 'Super Sprint' these events are held by clubs to encourage newcomers and often involve distances along the lines of a 200 m swim, a 10 km cycle and a 2 or 3 km run. If, like most people, it's the swim leg that worries you most then make sure that it is held in a swimming pool rather than open water. That way not only is it less threatening but you can also stand up any time you get tired. If you feel the splish is really getting on top of you then you can even walk the water stretch, if that's what works for you.

now there was an idea because surely some of those whizzy cyclists and runners would be weaker in the water. Some of them might even be as bad as me.

They were too. But even the doggy paddlers were breathlessly excited about triathlon so I ended up having a go. And still do.

You don't have to be a great swimmer. There are usually a few people cheerfully breast-stroking their way around the first leg. You don't have to be a great cyclist, as I prove regularly. Nor do you have to be a great runner, since triathlons come in all shapes and sizes and the shortest ones involve a run of as little as 3 km. The usual distances are:

- Sprint – in theory the sprint distance is half the 'Olympic' so a 750 m swim, a 20 km cycle and a 5 km run. In practice many sprints have swims that are half that length.

- Olympic – so-called due to its inclusion in the Olympics; this is the classic distance of a 1.5 km swim, a 40 km cycle and a 10 km run.

- Half ironman – getting scary now with 1.9 km of swimming, 90 km cycling and a 21.1 km (half marathon) run.

- Ironman – big bad and ugly; 3.8 km swimming, 180 km cycling and a full marathon to finish off. But you do get to go on about it for ever afterwards.

If the mix and match formula interests you but you just hate road racing then get off the road and wallow in the mud with Xterra – see IDEA 51, Xterra Xcitement.

Try another idea...

You'll need a swimming costume (or a pair of shorts you will wear throughout) and goggles, a bicycle and a helmet (this is essential, you can be disqualified for getting on the bike before putting your helmet on), and a pair of running shoes. When you arrive, you rack your bike by your number in the transition area ready for the first changeover (known as T1). Usually that's also where you return to for the second transition (T2) so your running shoes wait for you here, too. There may be a different transition area for T2 and the organisers will normally lay your shoes out for you there under your number. Other than that you just have to follow the pack, remembering that nudity is frowned on – so careful in T1 – and likewise 'drafting' (riding in the slipstream of another cyclist) is forbidden, so keep your distance. For every whippety, Lycra-clad, 'elite' man or woman trying to break records at the front of the pack you will find a handful of cheery have-a-goers like myself at the back simply out for a paddle, a peddle and a plod.

'If God invented marathons to keep people from doing anything more stupid, triathlon must have taken Him completely by surprise.'
Triathlon adage, attributed to one P.Z. PEARCE, M.D., sports medic

Defining idea...

How did
it go?

**Q   I got a really weird feeling of rubber legs in T2 – how do I avoid
that?**

A   *You need to get your body used to the transition from cycling to running.
You can practice doing 'bricks' (biking followed immediately by running) or
you can try standing on your pedals as you get to the end of the cycle to
get your legs used to bearing the weight again.*

**Q   I'm worried about this 'drafting' rule on the bike. How far should I
be from the next rider?**

A   *10 m, usually, but it does vary from event to event and the marshals are
likely to only tick people off if they are looking to deliberately gain
advantage. The penalty usually consists of a cooling-off period of a few
minutes where you have to stand and wait before being allowed to
continue.*

31

Circles in the sand – sandboarding

Carving arcs in the sand is an obvious alternative to snowboarding for those times when the temperature is above zero or you happen to want some board action on the beach.

The best thing is that even beginners pick it up fast and the skills you learn transfer to other board sports on snow or water.

The only catch with sandboarding is the lack of ski lifts. Other than that it is probably the best introduction to boarding of any kind. You don't need lots of expensive clothing (thick socks, sun block and a big smile normally cover it), and the only equipment involved is the sandboard itself. That said, a bit of safety gear can come in handy – skateboarding protections for your elbows or gloves, for example. Even though you are going to be boarding on soft dry sand (wet sand is too sticky for carving cool arcs) you can still leave a certain amount of skin behind if, like me, your principal board skill consists of spectacular and repeated wipeouts.

If you're a total newcomer and/or you find it hard enough keeping your feet even without a board strapped to them, you may want to ask about 'lying down' boarding. Strictly this isn't sandboarding so much as sledging but some places offer a fast route to the bottom using bigger boards that you lie face down on and then slide down the sand. There have even been experiments with sand scooters where

Carving curves is great but the time inevitably comes when you start to think about tricks, and the best way to get into tricks is to have a ramp. So build one. Not a permanent one of course, and nothing that will damage your pristine dune, but a temporary one can be built out of a sheet of plywood and some bags. The materials are light, and when you get to your site you turn the bags into sandbags by filling them up. Sand is free, it's there and you can dump it back again when you're finished (remembering to take the bags home with you, naturally). Then with a ramp in place you can start moving up to 'grabs' (grab the board with your hand as you go airborne), 360s (full helicopter turn in the air, land facing the same way as you start), and front flips (summersaults).

you sit down and grab the handlebars of what is basically a sandboard. To date, though, the conclusion seems to be that your classic sandboard remains the way to go if you want to twist and turn your way from top to bottom.

Sandboards are much like snowboards complete with bindings, but smarter sandboarders tend to go for lightweight boards simply because they know who has to carry them to the top of the dune each time. True, some boarders like to ride without bindings like a skateboard, but it's much better to have bindings, even fairly primitive ones, if you're hoping to carve curves and maintain control. There are fabulous professional boards available out there (check out the ranges at www.venomousboards.com, www.wideride.com or www.oceanculture.com), but not everybody can afford the luxury of a purpose-designed board. For those looking to 'convert' an old board or even make their own sandboard: don't be tempted to skip the bindings out of convenience. Even a simple bit of bungee cord will work wonders compared to no bindings at all.

Different types of dune hold more or less air between the grains of sand and so have different characteristics, so you may find that it pays to experiment with different styles of board for an area you surf regularly.

Experiment with weights and different degrees of upturn in the nose to find the physics that functions best. Early sandboards were slow and unwieldy but newer materials (humble Formica has proved a winner) and waxes mean that sandboarding can be as sedate or as speedy as you wish. Fast boards plus 'getting small' to minimise your wind resistance combine to bring a whole new meaning to the idea of 'quicksand'.

Quick note about that sand. Everyone's dream sandboarding location is Sosusvlei in Namibia where the world's highest (and reddest) dunes tower above you like the landscape of Mars and the dune faces are long and uninterrupted. Great stuff, but we can't all pop over to Namibia when the sandboarding urge takes us and have to make do with smaller coastal sand dunes. No problem with that on the fun stakes – any dune can be a fun dune – but look out for dune grass and plants. If there's greenery (or even brownery in hot climes) then go board somewhere else. Boarding around the dune grass risks damaging the roots (even if you can't see the damage) and, aside from showing due respect to Ma Nature, this ultimately means the dunes will disappear since the roots are what holds them together.

If sandboarding gets you stoked then IDEA 9, *Surfing on snow*, is soooooo you. Read on!

Try another idea...

'You always say "I'll quit when I start to slide," and then one morning you wake up and realize you've done slid.'
SUGAR RAY ROBINSON, forgetting to add that the thing to do next is to grab your board and run back up for another go

Defining idea...

How did it go?

Q **I tried it, I liked it and I'd like to take it more seriously – is there a competition circuit?**

A *Yup. Dune Riders International host the annual Sand Master Jam in the US and Action Sports dominates the European scene. Details of the World Sandboarding Championships (in Germany) can be found at www.sandboarding.org and DRI events are advertised on www.sandboard.com.*

Q **You mention making your own sandboard – any idea where I can get more details on that?**

A *Indeedy. The excellent Dr Dune has a fine article on precisely that subject which you will find at www.sandboard.com. Plus, you can always surf the sandboard websites and pinch ideas about dimensions.*

32

Paragliding

The purest form of flight? An aeroplane in a backpack? Or the art of dangling on strings from an oversized handkerchief? You decide.

Paragliding is pure physics, really, for all that it looks — and feels — like magic.

You and the glider are heavier than air and thus condemned to sink through it (hopefully not too quickly) until you meet the ground (hopefully not too painfully). However good the design of the wing it is only going to stay airborne if the column of air you happen to inhabit at that moment is rising away from the ground faster than you are falling towards it.

I remember the first time someone tried to explain that to me and I didn't really get it because all I was thinking was 'this man and I are about to jump off a mountain with only an oversized handkerchief and some string to keep us in the air'. At that point he could have been explaining that he knew we would fly because he'd heard it on a radio that he picked up via the fillings in his teeth. All that really sank in, and all that really mattered to me, was that if the rising/falling air equation did happen not to work out then at least I was hanging in a harness beneath a parachute, rather than a plane.

Here's an idea for you... **Try a tandem. Tandem flights are the best way to go for beginners because you can find out whether or not you like it without spending time learning about aerodynamics and meteorology. Even intermediates can still learn a lot from a tandem flight as it's the best chance you'll get to observe the experts from close up. They couldn't be simpler. Your pilot will lay out the glider, clip you into the harness and tell you when to run. You leg it, and before you know it your legs are still trying to run but you're not actually touching the ground. From there on you can relax and enjoy the view.**

Paragliding started out when parachutists in the Alps realised they could launch their new, square, steerable canopies from the ground and land in the valleys below. Since then they have come a long way and you don't have to have a handy mountain to take off. Ridge soaring and cliff hanging are still the easiest ways to get airborne but a really good pilot can ascend now in very light thermals. By using those, paragliding has gone from something you did off a mountain (landing lower down the same mount) to a means of flying long distances (flights of over 400 km have been recorded) across country by using the thermals. At least that's the theory; in practice it depends where you are. Countries with a lot of sun and large expanses of barren rock will produce dramatic and predictable thermals for cross-country work. Countries with large amounts of cloud and soggy grassland make pilots work that much harder. In some ways this may make them better pilots (and weather bores) since successful gliding in variable conditions requires a very fine knowledge of the slightest indicators of thermals – including the flight patterns of insects and birds in the take-off area.

It's easy to underestimate the amount of meteorological knowledge involved in flying successfully but on the plus side the physical controls are not as complex as you might think. One of the odder points about a paraglider is that you don't steer it like an aeroplane. Aeroplanes have control surfaces that provide fine touches to modify the aerodynamics. Paragliders have control lines that basically twist the shape of the wing so that it acts like a brake, slowing one side down more than the other in order to turn. Put simply it's the same principle as a tank or a bulldozer – you slow down one side enough for the other to overtake it. Yup, those effortlessly graceful, feather-weight flight craft can be thought of as sky tanks when it comes to turns.

Enjoyed this? Then check out IDEA 14, *Getting the hang of it.*

Try another idea...

One of the beauties of paragliding is that it's possible to cram wing, harness, control lines, et al. into a backpack which makes it easy to get to fairly remote launch points, fly to somewhere and pack everything back up again. One example of which is the launch site at Lion's Head in Cape Town, where paragliders walk up the footpath to the hilltop, launch off the side – and when they're done they land on the beach at Camp's Bay before packing the wing back into their rucksacks and heading into the bars. You try that with a Cessna.

'There is an art, or, rather, a knack to flying. The knack lies in learning how to throw yourself at the ground and miss. Pick a nice day and try it. All it requires is simply the ability to throw yourself forward with all your weight, and the willingness not to mind that it's going to hurt.'
DOUGLAS ADAMS, *The Hitchhiker's Guide to the Galaxy*

Defining idea...

137

How did it go?

Q **Love it to death and would like to learn the limits of my canopy and myself by moving on to trick flying (looping, anyone?). Any tips?**

A   *Yes, firstly make sure you seek out someone at your club or school who is already expert at what you want to try and make them run you through it over and over until your eyes glaze. Secondly do what all the test pilots do when they are testing a canopy's limit – do it over water so you're more likely to be wet and embarrassed than dead.*

Q **I want to be a qualified pilot but there seem to be several interpretations of what's involved. Why?**

A   *The International Pilot Proficiency Identification (IPPI) scheme has intermediate levels on the way to full pilot. While 'pilot' is often taken to mean IPPI level 4 there is also an intermediate IPPI level 3, equivalent to the British 'Club Pilot' which means that you are qualified to turn up to and fly from any other club. Different national systems have different names for levels but they are still IPPI equivalents. Check out what's relevant for you on the internet.*

33

Underground movements

Brits call it 'potholing', most enthusiasts call it 'caving' and kids call it 'spelunking' (then giggle a lot) but whatever name you give it caving will always exert a fascination over the select few.

After all, you get to go where few others have ever set foot.

Caving is definitely not for everyone. It tends to be cold, wet, muddy and claustrophobic. People will give you strange looks when you tell them what you do. There is no cool cavewear manufacturer, no good reason to wear expensive shades, dye your hair blond or show off your six pack. On the other hand you do see amazing things most other people never will and witness the natural sculptures of stalactites, stalagmites, helictites and flowstone.

Caves have their own fauna too, both in the form of trogloxenes (beasties that sleep, hibernate or roost in caves) and troglobies (beasties that live full time in the dark). Depending on where you are in the world caving can be an exercise in geological wonder or a subterranean safari in the quest for bats or exotic (and very slightly creepy) wonders such as the colourless and sightless amphibians that dwell in cave

There are commercial caves out there offering guided tours of grottoes or the entrances to systems but for a real taste of caving your best bet is to contact a local club (universities are often a good bet if you're having trouble finding one). Caving clubs are usually delighted to take newbies on a trip to their favourite sites and will be able to lend or rent you all the kit you need so you don't have to buy anything unless you're sure you will get good use out of it. Going the club route (or 'grottoes' as they're called in the States) means you get easy access to expertise, logistics and general organisation and can come back bragging merrily about not just getting off the beaten track but burrowing far beneath it.

waters. Caves are uniquely fragile places. Their ecosystems are often balanced on a knife-edge and even the seemingly solid formations of stone are extraordinarily delicate so an unthinking caver can wreck hundreds of years of development in a clumsy second. Don't be tempted to leave established routes or venture into unexplored caves unless you are a qualified speleologist. Not only could you do irreparable damage to these unique environments but caves are notoriously unforgiving of the reckless and quite capable of doing a fair amount of damage to you by way of return. Stick with an expert guide and make sure you're properly equipped.

This season's well-dressed caver is likely to be sporting all of the following:

- Lights. At least three of them in fact. The main light is usually mounted on a helmet, like a miner, leaving the hands free. You also need a backup, and a backup for the backup. All of them should be equally strong and all of them should have fresh batteries (you did check, didn't you?).

- A helmet – what else are you going to strap your helmet torch to?

If caving doesn't seem sufficiently claustrophobic or life-threatening then you could always go one better and delve into the world of IDEA 8, *Cave diving.*

Try another idea...

- Gloves and kneepads. Scrapes and cuts are no fun above surface, let alone in the bowels of the earth. Besides, what if the old films were right and you run the risk of emerging in a vast cave where dinosaurs still roam? You'll be grateful for all the protection you can get if you have to go mano a mano with pterodactyls.

- Rescue blanket – silver foil 'space' blankets fold down into a tiny square and can make all the difference in the battle against hypothermia.

- Dry, waterproof clothing – leave the cotton at home; it gets sweaty, then cold, then clammy.

- Boots. Leave the trainers at home too. Stumbling is easy to do underground and a solid boot that protects your ankle could well prevent you from becoming a limping liability that your teammates now have to get to the surface.

- Rubbish bag – everything that goes in with you comes out with you. That includes team members.

'Mind the gap.'
Passenger notice on the London Underground

Defining idea...

- Ropes and lines. While these aren't necessary for most popular caving trips they are often a good idea to have as a fallback if only to lay down a guideline to ensure a quick route to the exit. Remember that ropes are only as good as the person using them so if you are going to carry them you should also have learnt the appropriate rope skills.

Caving is a team sport, since soloists have a nasty habit of ending up as statistics. Make sure your team is the appropriate size (a large group in a small cave is a recipe for problems), has the appropriate experience and any necessary permission. Remember that the team extends beyond the people standing around you; make sure others know where you are, when you are due back and who to contact if you don't surface on schedule. Even though you're underground you are not immune to the weather so remember to check such key points as the weather forecast, recent rains and water levels in the caves.

How did it go?

Q How cold will it be?

A *Depends where you are. Caves in Cuba are reportedly toasty at about 20ºC but in the UK they tend to be under 10ºC. Get local information about the conditions before you dress to spend several hours in them.*

Q I've ventured into shallow, largely horizontal caves and would love to go further but am worried that I will need a lot of technical skills. Is that true?

A *Again it depends which caves you are thinking of. In the UK long and gentle limestone cave systems mean that it is possible to descend to a depth of 300 m without so much as touching a ladder or a rope.*

34

Abseiling and rap jumping

Absolutely *the* preferred method of getting down from tall buildings, cliffs and helicopters. As recommended by ninjas, special forces and self-respecting super-spies worldwide.

Abseiling is as easy as falling off a cliff...

No, now I come to think about it, that's not entirely true since falling off cliffs doesn't strictly require rope or bladder control, both of which are advisable when abseiling. On the plus side, however, that little bit of effort it takes to learn the ropes pays back big time in terms of being able to talk about the experience afterwards.

Abseiling (also called rapelling) can't really be described as a sport in its own right (although it often features in adventure racing) but it is a blast – sort of the grown-up version of sliding down banisters, and it takes far less strength or energy than you think. Abseiling is the art of sliding down a rope slowly, while fending off the wall/cliff face with your feet. The slowing down bit is done by a friction device attached to the rope – usually a simple 'figure of eight' loop that the rope runs through. That in turn is clipped onto a carabiner (snap-locking metal 'D' rings), which in turn clips onto your harness: a crotch-hugging belt and braces affair which would be entirely at home in your average S & M club. Many commercial abseils also have a safety rope clipped to your harness so that even if you were to throw the

Here's an idea for you...

Enjoy abseiling and want to try something a little more challenging? Easy. Turn over. Rap jumping was developed by the military as a means of abseiling out of helicopters, etc., while still being able to point and shoot at the bad guys below. For rap jumping the carabiner is clipped to the back of your harness and you just use one hand in front of you to feed the rope; the other one holds the Uzi/cigarette holder/champagne glass (depending on your personal style). At the top you lower 'into' the rope facing down so you are at right angles to the cliff, and then you start to 'run' down the face. The faster you can feed rope the easier it is to run or jump and oddly enough this makes the process much more stable than taking it slowly and trying to place your feet as you go. Not for the faint-hearted but tons of fun.

rope away and attempt to moondance in mid-descent you wouldn't go anywhere unexpected.

You start at the top of the cliff/wall with your back to the drop and balance on the edge before leaning back into the pull of the rope so that you are almost sitting off the cliff. Then you feed rope into the friction device and start to descend while your feet walk down the cliff face. Pulling the rope across the line of your body – behind your back for example – acts as an immediate brake. As you build confidence it becomes possible to feed the rope through faster and you can bound down the wall in a series of jumps as your feet push off and you let the rope through before coming back to the wall.

The exception to this is when the standard friction device is replaced by something altogether more genteel. For exceptionally high abseils, usually those over about 70 m, the friction can threaten to damage the rope and so a device called a 'rack' is used to slow it. The rack is like a barred gate with the rope threading in and out of the bars and the increased friction means that you really have to work at feeding the rope through it. This in turn means your bounding is replaced by a much more sedate pace. The advantages of that become clear at the higher abseils, such as the world's highest commercial abseil at Abseil Africa on Cape Town's Table Mountain. As you abseil down the 112 m of the drop from the 1000 m summit you suddenly realise that the cliff face drops away from you and you are left hanging twisting in mid air as you try to feed the rope through and descend to terra firma. It's a predicament known to the locals as 'dope on a rope'. It's also a fine test for the aforementioned bladder control.

Like altitude adrenalin and dangling off ropes? Sounds like a little tradding might be up your street. See IDEA 35, *Rad tradding*.

Try another idea...

'I'd like you to stand away from the edge when you're not roped up because I'm told that falling off cliffs really sucks.'
TIM, rap jumping instructor, Knysna, South Africa

Defining idea...

Q **As I step backwards off the cliff in abseiling my first couple of
steps inevitably leave me swinging wildly from side to side. Why?**

A *Your feet are too far apart at the start. As you lower yourself back into the
'sitting' position check that they are closer together and then your weight
will shift less to either side as you move and place each foot.*

Q **I tried rap jumping and my feet slithered off the rock in all
directions so I ended up dangling like a rear-mirror ornament. Can
this be right?**

A *Nope. Sounds as though you're trying to stand up so that you're vertical –
but since the rope is taking your weight your feet won't find good
purchase. Try to tense your stomach and trust the rope to hang so that you
are going down at right angles to the rock face and 'running' down the wall
rather than trying to stand on a vertical surface.*

35

Rad tradding

'Tradding' is climbing from the bottom up without having first inspected the route from above and without the use of pre-fixed anchor points or top ropes...

It is often considered the purist's climbing technique.

While sport climbing (using anchor points already provided in the rock face) is a great sport in itself, and can be fiendishly demanding, there is always that slight feeling that tradders (traditional climbers) hold the moral high ground. And very often the physical high ground too.

Of course, whenever there is any question of high ground there is also plenty of grumbling about details – is it still trad climbing if you have seen the rock from the top already? If you slip, does a purist tradder continue to use the anchor point that is now above you or do you have to start the route afresh? My own feeling is that if you even begin to care about any of that stuff then frankly you have too much time on your hands and should probably get out there and climb more.

The basic rule of tradding remains safety first (ropeless climbing is a truly extreme sport best left to the reckless few) and that means learning to fix 'protections' into the rock as you go. That's not to suggest power-drilling a hole and fitting a bolt, but instead using a number of devices such as 'chocks' and 'cams' which fit into natural

Here's an idea for you...

Do look down. No, not to scare yourself silly but because your feet are the key to strong climbing and it's a classic beginner's error to rely too much on upper body strength. We are vertical animals and our leg muscles are the powerhouses that support and propel us, so a good climb is all about getting the feet into position to push up, not on reaching up and pulling with the arms. By looking down you can compare hand and foot grips and in the beginning, at least, the chances are that when you're struggling it's because you've got a lovely clean handhold, but your feet are having to make do with uneven positions from which they can't propel you to the next step.

cracks and crevices and hold fast. They are in turn attached to your rope so that as you carry on climbing you can only fall as far as the last protection. Even though tradding doesn't involve setting a top rope for a belayer to hold you on, it's only sensible to learn your moves in the safety of a climbing gym with top ropes before getting out there and practising on the rock face itself.

Once out there for real you won't have the benefit of a top rope or fixed anchors and that in itself means you have to get a little more creative when it comes to techniques for taming the towers. Amongst others you may want to get your head and limbs around:

- Jamming – hands and fingers squeezed into cracks often give a better hold than normal grips.

- Advanced jamming – where cracks are too big for hands to jam in, but too small for the body, it's time to resort to more advanced jamming techniques such as the 'chicken wing' where a bent arm is squeezed into the crack and forced solid by trying to straighten the arm, with the palm pushing the shoulder into the rock face.

- Layback – where a grip is taken on a vertical crack and the body then leans in the opposite direction setting up a tension that holds you in place.

- Undercling is much like the layback but uses a hand grip the other way up (as if you were holding your palm out) and a lean out away from the rock.

- Crimping is where you get only a finger-tip hold or jam. Crimps put huge forces on the fingers so should only be a brief move to get into a better position.

- Smearing is when the foot gets a grip by bringing as much of the specialised rubber surface of the sole into contact with the rock face as possible.

- Chimneying is wriggling into cracks large enough to take your whole body and using your body as a jam so you can rest, grip and move up.

- Edging holds with the feet mean that you turn your foot sideways and set the edge of it into a crack or a thin ledge – far more effective than just resting your toes on it (a move called front-pointing).

Try another idea...

If tradding isn't challenging enough for you it's always possible to up the ante by learning to climb faces that are only temporarily solid. Learn more about ice climbing in **IDEA 15, *Swimming up solid water – ice climbing.***

Defining idea...

'Nobody climbs mountains for scientific reasons. Science is used to raise money for the expeditions, but you really climb for the hell of it.'
SIR EDMUND HILLARY

Don't be afraid to invent your own moves, however. Knees, bottoms and thighs may be frowned on as climbing aids by the purists but when you're out there on the rock face elegance comes a poor second to practicality. If your patented arse-jam is what gets you up there then you go ahead and boldly buttock-blaze your way to the summit.

How did it go?

Q **What's the difference between 'free' and 'aid' climbing and are they both forms of tradding?**

A *They can be, yes. 'Free' means that the climber makes it up the face with the strength of their limbs alone, and only has a rope present in case of falling. 'Aided' climbing means that the rope is used to help with the climb and is used for moves other than a pure safety backup.*

Q **What's the difference between top-roping and leading?**

A *Top-roping means you are held on belay by a partner on the ground, with a rope passing up through a point above you; lead climbing means starting from the bottom and setting protections as you go to reduce the risk of falling. The lead climber can anchor themselves at the top and belay the second person from above.*

36

Up, up and away

Parasailing/parascending is a short but sweet taster of soaring with no skill or experience required to 'solo'.

It has all the fun of flying without being strapped to an instructor.

Parasailing/parascending (the names are interchangeable) began back in the 60s as a means of training would-be parachutists about the feeling of flight. Now it has become a stunningly simple way of getting people up in the air and giving them a fun ride at anything up to an altitude of a couple of hundred metres. While it is possible to steer the 'chute the usual approach is to free the parasailor of responsibility for anything other than enjoying themselves, so parasailing really falls somewhere between a theme park ride and a sport.

The idea is simplicity itself. You are buckled up in a harness attached to both a parachute and a tow rope. The tow rope is attached to a boat, and when the boat accelerates across the water the parachute fills with air and soars aloft, taking you with it for a tethered ride above the earth, a bit like a balloon bobbing along on a string behind a skipping child. When the boat slows down you drop, but remember you are attached to a parachute so you aren't going to plummet back down. Just to be on the safe side parasailing is almost always done over water anyway.

Here's an idea for you...

Once you've mastered the basics you don't have to have a boat and a stretch of water for parascending. Although water is preferred for beginners the same effect can be achieved with a car – which is how the sport started out in the first place. After a brief struggle with the towing vehicle the pilot becomes airborne as usual, but since it is not usually convenient to have a car charging around towing a parachutist the land version of parascending is normally about getting the pilot sufficiently high so that they can release the tow rope and practice landing the 'chute themselves.

There are different variations on this theme, but the most commonly seen technique is called winchboat parasailing, and uses specially adapted boats with their own 'flight deck'. With a winchboat you can parasail over water without even getting your feet wet.

Step one is to stand on the flight deck (usually a small platform rather than something you'd try to put a helicopter down on) and strap into the body harness. Some operators use a chair harness, so you are pretty much sat down in a floating chair which is attached to the parachute, but most just strap you in so you are standing upright.

As the boat moves off your flight crew hold the parachute up so that it catches the wind. Called an HLLD canopy (High Lift, Low Drag), this is designed to inflate rapidly and lift as high as possible. As the canopy catches the air you are plucked off the deck and start to rise. How high you go depends on the length of the line and the speed of the boat but for a beginner's flight it's likely to be less than 100 m and the jaunt itself will probably last for five to ten minutes. At the end of the ride the winch simply reels the parasailor back down to the flight deck for landing, heroic tale-telling and cocktails.

Steering, if there is any to be done, is a question of pulling on the risers (the ropes that lead up to the canopy itself) to left or right, but with the slicker operators there is actually pretty much nothing to do aside from enjoying the view and working on your commentary for recounting the experience afterwards.

If you like being aloft under a canopy, then take a look at parachuting in IDEA 16, *Bailing out*.

Try another idea...

Variations on this theme include the beach take-off, where you start on the beach with the boat in the water pointing seawards. As the boat moves off you attempt to resist it to keep the line tight. This inevitably results in a kind of tug of war and unless you happen to win that war you will be pulled up and away as above. Although it may look as if the beach launch involves the pilot running for a start it is more a question of two or three steps as they resist the pull of the parachute, after which the ground just seems to fall away from your feet. You may be in for a wet landing from the beach start. The boat decelerates and you drift towards splashdown. Landing on land itself is possible but it takes a little more expertise, a touch more athleticism and is normally reserved for those with full-on parachute experience.

'The higher we soar, the smaller we appear to those who cannot fly.'
FRIEDRICH NIETZSCHE

Defining idea...

How did it go?

Q I'm sure I've seen this done with waterskis. Can I try it from a ski take off?

A   *It can be done with skis but you're unlikely to be offered that as, however exhilarating it is, it is quite demanding in terms of skills and landing in particular would need waterski jump experience. Plus, operators seem to have tired of having to go back and look for lost skis in the flight path.*

Q Can parasailing be done behind a jetski?

A   *Normal advice is for a boat with a 100 hp engine but modern jetskis do have the power to lift a parasailor. It's not considered a good idea, though, not least since jetski engines aren't designed to pull against that kind of drag for any length of time.*

37

Eat my wake

Wakeboarding is to waterskiing what snowboarding is to Alpine skiing, with the emphasis very much on carving cool curves and snapping out new tricks.

The great thing about board sports is that they feed off each other; if you like one, chances are you'll like another.

Skateboarding stole ideas from surfing, snowboarding cherry-picked tricks from skateboarding, surfing re-appropriated a few ideas from snowboarding and the whole merry cycle goes on with everyone learning from each other. It also means that if you've tried sandboarding/snowboarding/skateboarding you are immediately going to have a glimmer of an idea of what a wakeboard expects you to do in order to go anywhere. With one small difference, of course. Getting started on a wakeboard is not as simple as pointing your sand/snowboard down the hill. In fact the problem begins even before you get in the water.

Like snowboards, the bindings on a wakeboard work on the principle that it is better to be bound in than to fall off, and so they are normally adjusted so that nothing short of a high-speed wipeout or a small nuclear detonation is going to get them off. Of course that also means that they are a right pig to get on. Instead of trying to readjust them try reaching for the lube. Soap, 'Slime', or any other

Here's an idea for you...

Getting the hang of it? OK. So you can ride the board now with no problem and you're starting to get the idea of spins, rolls and flips in the air but you can only perform the simple stuff and don't see a way of moving on. Shake your brain up a bit by riding 'switch' (backwards). Just like learning to rollerblade backwards it's all a matter of learning to initiate the same moves but in reverse. Start on dry land by standing on your board and thinking through the way you're going to have to move in order to meet the wake with your body going the other way.

biodegradable lubrication will do, just fight shy of oils and petroleum gels which will rot the binding (and wetsuits, of course). The rule of thumb (toe?) is that however tight they feel, your bindings aren't too tight unless they actually make your feet go numb.

Now you're in the water holding the rope handle (palms down) and waiting to go. Thinking a little about your body position will help a lot here – bring your shoulders back and your chest out like a trooper on parade and drop your knees out sideways slightly so your straight arms reach forwards between them. Keep your knees bent – they're about to absorb a lot of force. The idea is that as the boat moves off the board will start to plane across the surface of the water and you will naturally rise up on top of it. That's the idea.

In reality I'm guessing that you will soon become familiar with these:

- The plough. Boat's off, water's rushing by, but you seem to be on your back, board sticking up like a gravestone, seemingly intent on ploughing a furrow rather than catching air. If that happens it means the water isn't going under the board and it can't plane. Try to push the nose of the board down with your front foot and straighten your feet to bring the board surface flatter on the water.

- The side slide. 'I'm up, I'm up – and I'm going sideways.' This is usually followed quite quickly by a face-down crash (which I prefer to see as the first trick rather than a painful confrontation with rushing water). The nose of the board should be pointing in the direction the boat is going, not at the boat itself. Sideways slipping on any board is usually due to torso positioning – remember you turn by twisting your shoulders and upper body, so you're probably pointing your upper body at the boat not where you want to go.

If you've come from a skiing, rather than a boarding background, then waterskiing may be a better way for you to start – see IDEA 10, *An elephant can do it.*

Try another idea...

- 'I'm up, I'm up... look at the speeding water. Look at it getting closer. Look at me crashing face down into the wake.' Snowboards, in-line skates, you name it, will all pretty much go where you are looking because you tend to angle your shoulders towards the thing you are looking at. So if you look down you're going to go down. It's hard not to stare at the burbling white water beneath you but believe me you're going to come face to face with it quite often enough without looking for a meeting.

Once you're up the idea is to ride over the towing boat's wake, effectively using that as a ramp to launch you in the air, which is your chance to perform rolls, flips – and spectacular crashes.

'You must live in the present, launch yourself on every wave, find your eternity in each moment.'
HENRY DAVID THOREAU

Defining idea...

How did
it go?

Q **I'm watching where my shoulders go and yet I still go into the side slide of death almost as soon as I rise up onto the water. Why?**

A *Could be that you're thinking about your shoulders but still pulling the handle towards your navel instead of the lead hip. This isn't waterski so you're sideways on, not facing dead forwards, and pulling the handle to your belly will result in a twisting force which in turn leads to the side slide of death.*

Q **I've got it, I'm good at it and I'm getting into tricks, but I'm completely flummoxed about what flips and rolls are since my idea of a roll seems to be the instructor's idea of a flip. Why?**

A *Tricks in boarding are described in relation to the board, not the rider, so when the rider tucks their head in and performs a forward summersault the board rotates side over side. which is called a roll. Flips are when the board rotates end over end.*

38

Reach for the sky

Hang gliding and paragliding may have revolutionised the sport, but those with a taste for performance, not to mention total silence, will always prefer to do their soaring in sailplanes.

For some, soaring is more akin to meditation than sport.

Once gliding meant aeroplanes without engines, but hang gliding muddied those waters and so now a lot of gliding aficionados refer to their sport as soaring and their craft as sailplanes. If you've never seen a glider close up you will be amazed by their fine lines and sculpted elegance; long thin wings sprout from a thin fuselage and an aerodynamic, teardrop cockpit holds the pilot. These are the catwalk models of aviation. They are also completely silent, since they don't have engines, and the closed cockpit ensures that the pilot's tranquillity is not wiped out by the rush of wind.

Once aloft, even their elegant aerodynamics would condemn gliders to come back down to earth if it wasn't for the cunning exploitation of natural 'lift' in air patterns.

Here's an idea for you...

If you want to be good at gliding you'll have to learn to read the air patterns – otherwise you won't find thermals and ridge lifts and your flights will be embarrassingly short. There are many indicators of thermals and air movement but few are as good as clouds so go learn the difference between your nimbus and your stratus. For example 'cotton wool' cumulus clouds tend to form above thermals, while cigar-shaped lenticular clouds may be the tell-tale sign of a wave lift in the making.

There are three main air patterns that gliders can use to gain altitude and prolong their flight; thermals, ridge lift and wave lift.

■ Thermals are columns of rising air that form over heat sources, such as factories or rocky outcrops warmed by the sun. If you've ever seen flakes of ash floating in the hot air above a fire then you've seen thermal flying. By circling in a thermal the glider can rise and then use that altitude to glide to the next thermal in the direction of travel. Knowing where thermals are involves a good understanding of geography, meteorology and the clues that nature provides, including weather systems and bird behaviour.

■ Ridge lift is where a wave of wind hits a hill and flows up the face, so being directed straight up in the air.

■ Wave lift also comes about because of the wind blowing against a hillside but the air then flows over the hill, comes back down to earth and bounces off it to rise back up again. That bounce may then come back down to earth and bounce again, effectively making a ridge lift wind carry on for kilometres and end up nowhere near the original hill. The Andes is a classic spot for wave lift and it was wave lift that helped set the gliding distance record of 2463 km as well as the height record of 15,000 m.

Of course all of this means nothing if you can't get the engineless planes off the ground and into the air. The gentlest way of getting airborne is by hitching a ride from a powered plane. A tug plane takes off with a cable attached to the glider and the two rise together. When the desired altitude is reached the glider pilot releases the cable and the soaring starts. That tends to be a little expensive, however, and there is a cheaper option which is to use a winch. Again the glider is hooked up to a tow cable but the other end is connected to a powerful winch which reels it in rapidly, accelerating the glider down the runway and hauling it up and into the air like a kite before the pilot releases the cable. The third, and least common, is perhaps the most spectacular. Believe it or not it is possible to launch a glider by bungee – just like the little toy gliders you may have fired into the air with rubber bands when you were a kid. The glider is perched on top of a hill and a huge bungee attached to the tow hook. Teams of runners then charge off with the other end and the plane is catapulted off the ground into the ridge lift, which takes it skywards. At least that's the theory. Unsurprisingly there aren't that many pilots who opt for the bungee take-off these days. There is one other alternative which remains rare – the self-launching motorglider which has a fold-away engine that can be used for the launch and then folded back into the glider once in the air.

> **Fancy soaring free but prefer to do it featherweight style? Check out hang gliding; see IDEA 14,** *Getting the hang of it.*
>
> *Try another idea...*

While low clouds, heavy rain and very strong winds are all enough to stop gliders from flying, the different means of take-off and lift source means it doesn't have to be a beautiful summer's day to fly and you don't often have to book in advance. So if you want to glide with grace and style why not simply roll up to the nearest club and ask to have a go?

> *'No bird soars too high, if he soars with his own wings.'*
> WILLIAM BLAKE
>
> *Defining idea...*

161

How did it go?

Q **I took a tandem flight and now want to learn to fly gliders but how long will I have to fly before I can go solo?**

A *In theory you need twenty flights before you can go solo, though that will be waived if you have a pilot's licence. In practice, however, most people require up to double that number before they're comfortable enough to have a go themselves.*

Q **I'm a big bloke – is that a problem?**

A *It might be. Weight is an issue and many gliders have maximum weights and passenger heights (those cockpits aren't very big) but it is always worth asking at the club if they can take you.*

Q **Do I need a licence?**

A *Not in the UK, but outside of the UK (or as a UK pilot going abroad) you may well need one, depending on the country. Check out the regulations for where you will be flying on the Web.*

39

White-water rafting

Bucking and bouncing down roaring water in an inflatable raft is like a fairground ride with knobs on.

Exhilarating it may be, but fail to respect the river and danger will lurk beneath the surface.

White-water rafting is a huge growth sport with many different variations and degrees of difficulty. For some it is enough to sweep along the river and feel the speed and power of the water, others want to be part of a team paddling when told to in order to clear obstructions and get round bends. More extreme rafters are after a full-on slalom experience, preferably tumbling down a few waterfalls on the way.

Because there are so many different approaches to it there is an international grading system for rapids to try and help you understand what you are letting yourself in for.

RAPID GRADING

- Grade 1: easy – fast water with waves but no real obstructions.
- Grade 2: easy – but challenging for newbies. Rapids require some manoeuvring.

Here's an idea for you...

When rafting in the smaller inflatable canoe-style rafts you'll spend a fair amount of time trying very hard to steer in between the rocks and the hard places. In doing so you may just be getting yourself into more trouble than you need. In many cases if you really, really want to miss a rock then what you should do is aim straight for it. As the water pounds into a rock it is thrown back and round it, creating a protective wash of white water immediately around the obstacle like a very soggy force field. Point straight at the rock and the river itself will sweep you round it.

- Grade 3: not easy – needs coordination and/or a decent skipper. Rapids tend to be noisy and may have a mix of rocks, currents and bends to negotiate.
- Grade 4: difficult – wild water with surprises in store.
- Grade 5: expert – long, violent and unpredictable with genuine dangers.
- Grade 6: almost impossible – extreme water with a high risk of death or serious injury.

Be careful about the above, however, since grading something as variable as water is hit and miss. What seems like an easy course can turn into real danger if the paddlers make a stupid mistake and get caught in backwash; a difficult course can be made simple with a little local instruction. Any can be affected by variations in visibility or water level. Until you can truly consider yourself an expert it makes sense to stick with local operators and ask their advice. You can also get a pretty fair hint from the type of craft they use to get down the rivers.

RIGS

A rig is a huge raft consisting of a number of inflatable pontoons held together with frames and often equipped with an outboard motor. If the operator uses a 'rig' then

White water got you in a whirl? Try white-water kayaking – **IDEA 42, *Wild-water and white-water slalom.***

Try another idea...

you're probably in the Grand Canyon or Fraser River of the US; you're not going to tip over no matter what and you're not going to learn a huge amount about rafting since frankly whatever you do personally will make little difference.

PADDLE RAFT

These are seen pretty much anywhere fresh water manages to raise a ripple. The crew (that's you) sit along the sides, usually with a couple of stronger paddlers in the bows, while the skipper sits in the stern and steers with an oar. Your job is to be the engine, paddling when told to. Aside from stopping and starting, the main skills you're likely to learn are how to lean forwards to throw the raft's weight front on into waves, and lean sideways to 'high side' as you take on waves side on.

INFLATABLE CANOES/KAYAKS

These can be one or two man, and are highly buoyant sit-in canoes either open, in the case of canoes, or with a sealed deck in the case of

'No man ever steps in the same river twice ... all is flux, nothing stays still.'
HERACLITUS

Defining idea...

kayaks. The canoes are excellent for longer river trips or touring where white water is expected. The kayaks have a reputation for being able to take pretty much whatever is thrown at them and are increasingly popular for the hairy stuff. In both you are much lower on the water and will be able to see its behaviour close up.

BODY BOARDS AND HYDROSPEEDS

Body boards are small surfboards, hydrospeeds are a sort of water-borne bobsled invented by the French. These mean you are going to get seriously wet and will probably be spat down a rockless flume like a very high speed water slide.

INFLATABLE INNER TUBES

Fun, easy, and a huge laugh for the lower grade rapids. No skills required.

HYDRO-BRONC

You're going rafting in hydro-broncs? Wow. Also known as wheelfrafts, these are basically big balls of inflated tubes piloted by running and leaning inside like an outsized hamster in a beach ball. They are really hard work but naturally protect their occupants. Hydro-broncs are about the only thing that can safely take on Grade 6 rapids.

Q **I enjoy rafting in the inflatable kayaks but seem to ping down the river like a pinball, barely out of one problem before the next one is spitting me out. Any ideas?**

How did it go?

A *Did you start your rafting in larger rafts with someone shouting orders? If so you may be used to a more heads-down approach, paddling like fury and dealing with the hazard to hand. In the smaller rafts you need to act more like a skipper yourself. Fix your vision on the river 50–100 m ahead and focus a little more on planning for what is to come rather than what's right in front of you.*

Q **Our last skipper kept referring to 'hydraulics'. Isn't everything in the river hydraulic?**

A *'Hydraulic' is another name for a 'hole' and it means a point where water pours over a drop and momentum sends it charging down to the river bottom. Because that creates a dip in the water level, more water charges into the hole to fill it; since that water usually comes from downstream it results in a strong backflow where the surface water flows against the current.*

40

Extreme Ironing – ironing in the soul

The appeal of Extreme Ironing is simple – all the excitement of extreme sports combined with the undeniable satisfaction of an impeccably pressed shirt.

You might think that laundry and living on the edge are not obvious soul mates, but you'd be wrong...

When Extreme Ironing founding father Phil Shaw decided to break out the extension cord into the back garden for a little al fresco ironing it was to prove the inspiration for a movement that has inspired athletes around the globe. From out of the thriving, thrill-seeking spot of Leicester, England sprang up a hardcore body of Ironists such as 'Starch', 'Fe', 'Short Fuse', 'Flex' and 'Basket' who together formed the Extreme Ironing Bureau – the sport's governing body. First, Leicester – next, the world, has been the story to date and Extreme Ironing has built up a following in countries as far afield as Japan, Holland, the US, South Africa, Germany and New Zealand. The first world championships took place in Munich, Germany in 2002 and it can only be a matter of time before the Olympic Committee meets to consider the sport's inclusion in the Olympic Games. Big money sponsorship and extended TV coverage is poised in the wings.

Here's an idea for you...

Taking Extreme Ironing forwards is a constant challenge. Some of the great achievements remain tantalisingly out of reach; for example, while Base Camp has been ironed, no Ironist to date has been photographed chasing out the crumples at the summit of Everest. Somewhere out there is a budding Ironist just waiting to scale that pinnacle of human achievement.
Take a look at the Extreme Ironing website – www.extremeironing.com – and check out the picture gallery; see if there are any gaps you think you are best suited to fill. It might be ironing in a particular location, or it might be that nobody has yet combined the purity of Extreme Ironing with your own preferred adventure sport (heli bungee ironing, anyone?). The opportunities are legion, and the chance to become a legend in laundry is there for the taking.

The joy of Extreme Ironing is that it offers a challenge to the imagination, while proving the perfect antidote to the self-reverential 'radical dude' culture that can sometimes dominate adventure sports. The various 'disciplines' or styles of Extreme Ironing gently mock the tribalism of adventure sports in general. Extreme Ironing refuses to take itself seriously, it focuses on fun above all else (well, above everything except perfect creases), and anyone can have a go anywhere. The limit is you.

Extreme Ironing variations include urban style, forest style (ironing up trees), rocky style (many of the original Ironists were mountaineers), and water style (legendary Ironist 'Iron Lung' helped get scuba ironing on its way). Ironists have been photographed ironing on top of rocky spires, diving under ice (be aware that garments often freeze on surfacing), hanging upside down off Tyrolean traverses, and BASE jumping off cliffs. Attempts have been made to chase out creases in a single pass while the Ironist flies past (whether propelled by trampoline or motor vehicle) and there are discussions afoot for high-speed ironing in which Ironist and board might meet briefly while moving in different directions.

In competition marks are given for adventurousness, style, speed, difficulty and, of course, quality of pressing. The international judges are known for their severity but there are plenty of opportunities for trade-offs, for example sacrificing quality of pressing or speed for a particularly tricky move (while sky surfing out of a plane, for example). Phil Shaw ('Steam') has also gone on to establish different categories of iron ranging from the 'One Iron' – the heavyweight class of 1800 to 2000 watts, through to the 'Four Iron' – travel irons – not great for stubborn creases, but the tool of choice for anytime, anywhere, opportunist Ironing. There really are no limits, although some safety rules have become established, including avoiding electric irons when attempting Extreme Ironing feats underwater or in raging torrents. Interestingly, while Extreme Ironing is often performed as a team sport, there seem to have been few attempts at synchronised Ironing – whether in the water or in freefall. Surely that represents an opportunity for budding Ironists somewhere in the world?

Try another idea...

There is no shortage of ways forward for those interested in Extreme Ironing, but if you are particularly intrigued by the offbeat side of off-road adventuring then take a look at **IDEA 48,** *World Wide Weird.*

Defining idea...

'Ask a mountaineer why he or she climbs, they often answer "because it's there". An extreme ironist irons his or her clothes "because they're creased".'
PHIL SHAW, aka 'Steam', explains the philosophy behind the sport

How did it go?

Q   Do I have to carry a conventional ironing board with me?

A   *If your intention is a striking photo then purists would argue that the Ironing moment is not complete without a proper folding ironing board (preferably with one of those mini-me attachments for sleeves). It's a broad-minded sport, however, so variations on the theme have included using surfboards, snowboards or even other Ironists as the basis for Extreme Ironing moments.*

Q   My ironing is coming on a storm but I'm worried that I'm overemphasising my physical development to the detriment of my spiritual side. Can you help?

A   *Your concern is undoubtedly legitimate but fortunately the spiritual side of Extreme Ironing also has its devotees. In particular the German Ironists have combined ironing and yoga to come up with the soothing and harmonious activity of Eso-Ironing, check it out at www.extremeironing.de.*

Q   Does my iron have to be plugged in?

A   *The invention of the cordless travel iron has truly liberated linen from the laundry room and man from the shackles of humdrum existence. Look to battery power – and liberty.*

41
Scare yourself witless with SCAD

What could be more buttock-clenching than bungee? Bungee without the rope, that's what, and that's basically what SCAD (supposedly from Suspended Catch Air Device) diving is all about.

SCAD diving started out in Germany and originally involved jumping out of helicopters.

Nothing too unusual there. Pushing people out of helicopters has been the sport of choice for repressive regimes for decades, but in this case the jumpers are voluntary, indeed paying, and the landing is softened somewhat by the presence of a safety net. In many parts of the world (including the UK) pushing people out of helicopters is still frowned upon by public safety bodies, even with the promised net, and so SCAD operators such as Drop Zone have turned to fixed drop systems, usually letting you fall from about 50 m up. SCAD systems can usually be found at fairs but there are year-round sites and the likes of Drop Zone will be more than happy to arrange events (see www.dropzoneuk.com).

Of course there's a little more to it than simply being chucked down from a great height. You start by being togged up in a CFF (Controlled Free Fall system) harness,

Here's an idea for you... **Can't get yourself onto a helicopter but still looking for more? While the CFF harness and the SCAD net do serve to eliminate any risk, including those from hot-head heroics on the way down, it is possible to make the experience just a little bit more 'out there' by picking your time carefully. As with pretty much any jump (bungee and parachuting included) opting to do it at night will turn up the adrenaline volume nicely if you think that the standard version is a little too tame for you (tiger!).**

not unlike a paragliding harness. The CFF limits your movement and ensures that you will fall in a safe position for landing. Sadly for glory seekers this 'safe' position happens to be bottom first, so there are no chances for swan dives or back flips on the way. You can wriggle like a worm on a hook (and that's curiously how you'll feel) but you can't change your position once you're in the CFF.

Then you're off, hoiked upwards in a cage attached to a crane. There's a hole in the floor of the cage and it doesn't take long to figure out what that's for. To keep you company you have an operator who'll probably ask you some sort of stupid question like 'ready?' to which you can answer whatever you like because you don't get much choice in the matter from here on. The operator gives you a countdown and hits the release. And that's it. Gravity takes its course and you plummet in total freefall, without anything holding you back.

Just before you meet your maker you hit the safety net. If you're thinking of trapeze artists hitting the net and rebounding up again then think again. The net in this case is where SCAD gets its name as the Suspended Catch Air Device uses air tubes and brake suspensions linked to the double net. It looks like a big square inflatable swimming pool with netting for a bottom. The result of which is that the fall is soft, more like plunging into a vast marshmallow than hitting a trampoline. When you're safely stopped the net is lowered to the ground and, jelly legs permitting, you are free to get up and stagger off to the pub to tell everyone about your heroism. While you're at it don't forget to mention that you will have accelerated up to about 105 km/h in the two and half seconds the fall lasts.

Professional SCAD divers don't use the same harness as us mortals and are free to perform acrobatics like any other high divers. The ultimate is still considered to be the helicopter dive and, local laws permitting, this can still be arranged in a number of countries worldwide. If you're trying to find out where you can have a go then try contacting the inventors, MONTIC Hamburg of Germany, who can be found at www.montic.de.

If you get a feeling for freefall, and want to take it all the way then the ultimate thrill is undoubtedly BASE jumping: check out IDEA 13, *Back to basics*, for more.

Try another idea...

'Fall down seven times; stand up eight times.'
Japanese Proverb

Defining idea...

How did it go?

Q **Whoa, hold up there, I'm seventy, is this a good idea?**

A *As good an idea as anything else that involves flinging yourself from heights. You won't be the oldest and the impacts involved are less than those of bungee or parachuting, both of which are done by all ages.*

Q **Great. I'm also 140 kg in weight – any problems with that?**

A *I have a policy of never arguing with someone who weights 140 kg. Besides the maximum safe limit is 150 kg so you've got a few more pies to scoff before you can count yourself out on that basis.*

Q **What if a rope breaks or I miss the net?**

A *SCAD is patented and its specifications are very exacting. Each rope has to be tested to take up to ten times the maximum weight it is expected to bear, and the system works on triple redundancy – so not only is there a backup, but the backup has a backup. About missing the net: you don't really want to do this, do you? You yourself can't miss the net, that could only happen if the SCAD and drop were set up wrongly. So the answer is simple. Never go first. If the first bloke stands up and smiles then join the queue. If he doesn't, then save your money for the dodgems.*

42

Wild-water and white-water slalom

If a downhill ski race was run in and out of boulders it would be called madness...

For wild-water and white-water kayakers, however, racing downhill around rocks and hard places is all part of the fun.

Any downhill racing in white water requires strong paddling skills, the ability to read the river ahead and to turn and brace (a paddle move that keeps you from tipping over) in order to avoid being flipped by the eddies and currents around obstacles. It also requires helmets, flotation vests and a mean Eskimo roll ready for those times when the river gets the better of you. Which it will.

If you can put a tick by all the above then perhaps it's time to up the adrenaline quotient a little and try your hand at competition. Competition is seen as the fastest route to honing your skills and the joy of kayaking and canoeing is that there are so many different ways of competing. Racing isn't just about speed. There are plenty of different ways of putting yourself and your craft through the mill. Some rely on long distance endurance, others on strength and handling skills or the ability to

Here's an idea for you...

Looking for a fun way to improve your manoeuvring and paddling skills? Then look no further than canoe polo. This is basically water polo, played in a pool, and shooting for a metre-square goal suspended 2 m above the surface at each end. You play in BAT (Baths Advanced Trainer) kayaks, which are small and round-ended, and you can block the shots with hand or paddle. It can get fast and frenzied and you will have to twist and turn around other BATs to get to the ball. Single-minded focusing on the ball, combined with attempts at extreme turns and bracing action, mean that you will also get to perfect your rolling because sooner or later you're going to end up looking up at the pool bottom.

read the river and choose the best line. Then there's rodeo, effectively a virtuoso display of stunt canoeing.

Slalom racing involves making it through a series of 'gates' in the right order, a little like downhill skiing slaloms except that a) getting through the gates involves going upstream as well as down and b) the course is strewn with rocks and obstacles. Miss a gate, or take it in the wrong direction, and you get penalties. Every boat gets two runs at the course. Fastest time, penalties included, wins.

Wild-water races are against the clock and purely downstream. The skill is to pick the line down a white-water course (hint: any line that involves going through or over the boulders is likely to be sub-optimal). The fastest time wins, simple as that. Special wild-water boats can be used which are long, sleek and tippy like sprint canoes, but decked over and paddled by kneeling. The result is a hell-for-leather charge through the spray interspersed with desperate attempts not to wind up wrapped around a rock.

Marathon races can involve any kind of canoe and pretty much any kind of distance – the longest ones take several days. Don't be surprised if the race organisers have deliberately chosen routes which mean that sometimes you will have to get out and carry the damn thing; you may want to bear that in mind when choosing the boat for the job. You usually have pretty much a free hand on the style of boat, whether Indian canoes or Eskimo-style kayaks, so you can find the race to suit you and your craft. On the plus side, marathon races are also some of the most scenic ways of exploring long river stretches in the company of a horde of like-minded paddlers, and while the leaders may be flat out for victory there is usually a healthy back-of-pack group in it for the fun, the ride and the views.

If river canoes and kayaks are your thing, but competition isn't your bag, then take a look at IDEA 29, *Paddle your own canoe.*

Try another idea...

Rodeo is about as completely insane as it gets in a boat. Rodeos take place in a hydraulic (also called a 'hole') in a river – which means a spot where the water naturally plunges over a drop, forming a dip which is then instantly filled by more water rushing to it. The whorls and eddies can be fierce and that's what the rodeo rider exploits to perform flips and spins, often standing their kayak on end to do so. Paddlers are scored on the basis of their artistry and boat control. And not drowning, naturally.

'Well, the principle seems the same. The water still keeps falling over.'
SIR WINSTON CHURCHILL, when asked whether the Niagara Falls looked the same as when he first saw them

Defining idea...

How did it go?

Q   Why do rodeo and other 'play' boats ride so low in the water?

A   *So-called 'low-volume' kayaks are less buoyant and easier to tip which makes it possible to perform tricks, such as bow stalls, where you effectively slam the brakes on so hard that the boat stands upright on its nose in the water.*

Q   I reckon I'm pretty fast and fancy a go at wild water – is there any technique I should focus on before I sign up?

A   *Yes, the various forms of bracing – because against the clock you will inevitably take routes through rougher water than you might if you were taking your time. Braces – the paddle strokes that stop you tipping over – will be essential to stay upright and make it to the finish.*

43

Freefall fandango

Take a team of synchronised swimmers and drop them out of a plane 4000 metres up. You know you want to.

Just to make it more interesting shove a cameraman out with them, allow the option of surfboards as accessories and that's pretty much what freestyle skydiving is all about.

Simply making it to earth after falling from a plane has long been considered kids' stuff. Some skydivers clearly get so bored during those long descents that they have taken to amusing themselves with gymnastics, dance moves, team moves and even, heaven forbid, surfboards. The artistry lies not just in what the individual athlete can perform but in how they interact with the camera, itself placed on the helmet of another freefaller. Rather than concentrate on preventing themselves from burying themselves in the ground that cameraman/woman twists and turns, cavorting round the freefaller to get the best shots. Since there is always the risk that either the freefaller or the cameraperson may well get carried away with their

Here's an idea for you...

If you're an experienced skydiver and you're looking to try any of the above then the first stage is to try traditional formation jumping. Formation jumping is the stuff you've seen ever since you were a kid and you were taken to see military parachuting teams. As the divers drop they form up in the sky and take hold of each other's wrists/ankles, etc., to form concentric patterns prior to deploying their parachutes. While it may seem a little tame compared to the above it still works on the same basis of airspeed and directional control plus tight teamwork, and forms an excellent basis for moving on.

performance, rather than their plummet, it is usual for freeflyers to use an Auto Activation Device (AAD) which deploys both of their parachutes at the same time. As well as taking account of artistic distraction during descent this is also necessary because, with each freefaller travelling at speeds approaching 200 km/h, any collision can very easily mean concussion. Freestyle and sky surfing are definitely not for the beginner but if they do sound like your idea of fun, here's what it's all about.

FREESTYLE

Freestyle skydiving involves an individual going through a range of dance/gymnastic moves while upside down, rightways up, spinning, twisting – absolutely anything you like, in fact. As such it is entirely open to individual interpretation, however muscular or balletic that may be. Since it involves no special equipment or teamwork it is the least complicated of the extremes of freefall but international standards and a well-established competition circuit make it very challenging for newcomers to make their mark.

SKY SURFING

The sky surfer exits the plane with a surfboard attached to their feet and then performs acrobatics which are recorded by a freefalling cameraman/woman. The camerawork is considered as much a part of the overall performance as the freefaller and so the flying camera and the freefaller will have worked out a complex choreography of moves to get the most dramatic angles of each surfing twist or curve. Originally the boards were simply surf or boogie boards but they have since been developed with quick-release bindings and lighter materials to help with control up in the clouds.

FREEFLYING

Although skydivers would doubtless not appreciate the synchronised swimming comparisons this is basically what it's all about. In freeflying a number of freestyle jumpers complete synchronised and coordinated moves as they fall. These range from the balletic to the downright comic – with, for example, a line of freeflyers apparently attempting to run away from each other in mid air, or acting as each other's reflection. Anything goes, but tight choreography and teamwork are the hallmarks and have more in common with dance than diving (accompanying tantrums and hissy fits, if they do happen, are kept firmly under wraps).

If airborne lunacy is your thing and you have enough freefall jumps to your name then the only real place to go from here is BASE jumping. See IDEA 13, *Back to basics – BASE jumping*, for more but don't say I didn't warn you.

Try another idea...

Defining idea...

FREEFALL FLYING

This one definitely gets filed under 'hmm'. Freefallers have experimented for some years now with ways of increasing their glide factor. This has usually meant webbed gloves and 'wings' of material between arms and body giving the overall impression of what a superhero would look like if they had to go through a tadpole stage on the way to adulthood. Felix Baumgartner, however, had to go one better. In 2003 he strapped on a purpose-built carbon-fibre wing, jumped from a plane over England (about 9,000 m over England to be precise), and didn't pull his ripcord until he was over France (some 35 km later). For some this is the future of skydiving. For others it is the best argument for Club Class in years.

Q **So can I jump with a snowboard and bindings?**

A *Not recommended. Although most of the boards used by sky surfers do now resemble snowboards they are noticeably different, not least in having quick release bindings intended to dump the board in the air (and in a hurry) if anything goes wrong.*

Q **Any tips on controlling freefall when upside down?**

A *I believe you need to work on your olav frog. Best thing would be to go find someone who can demonstrate that slightly more convincingly than I could.*

How did
it go?

44

Sea kayaking

Slicing gently through the waves with no sound other than the gentle slap of paddle sliding into water...

One of the greatest ways of feeling close to the ocean without actually ending up in it. Hopefully.

Sea kayaking gets you close to things you might never otherwise approach. It is possible to kayak with killer whales, paddle with penguins or splash along with sea lions. My own favourite moment was when all the bored fur seals on a Namibian beach left in one huge, hairy sealalanche and tumbled into the water only to reappear all around my boat, turning cartwheels and launching themselves clean over the kayak. Well, most of them made it clean over. One landed flat on the deck leaving it and me staring at each other in mutually be-whiskered bewilderment.

You don't have to have the wildlife cameo appearances to appreciate the beauty of sea kayaking, however. The simple pleasure of slicing gently through the waves under your own near-silent power is astonishingly soothing. Kayaks are a lot more stable than they look, and while true mastery takes time, simply getting a grip on the skill of kayaking takes mere minutes, so it is an excellent sport for perfectionists and perfect beginners alike. Be warned, though. If you're not used to paddling as a means of transport then you may find it surprisingly tiring. A couple of hours is

Some people seem to be able to cruise smoothly all day and others get tired in minutes. Personal fitness aside, a lot of this is down to stroke efficiency so whether you're an improver looking to get faster, or a beginner looking to save energy it pays to paddle straight. Just because you've got a rudder it doesn't mean that you should be using it all the time to correct the imbalance in your stroke. Instead aim to place the paddle as close to the side of the kayak as you can and keep the stroke in line with the centre line of the boat. Movement out to the side will create a greater turning force which you then have to counterbalance, wasting energy in the process. The more you put the paddle in to the water out to the side the greater the turning force. Another way to try and learn good habits is to insist on a shorter paddle. Try it and see how much energy you save from creating less turn in your stroke.

usually more than enough for most beginners so don't sign up for that full day outing without trying a shorter jaunt first.

Since sea kayaks usually have more room to manoeuvre in than their fresh-water siblings they don't need to be so manoeuvrable, which means they can be more stable. They tend to be longer, leaner and with a tail rudder operated by foot pedals which rather conveniently means that you press right to turn right, and left to turn left. If you don't happen to have a rudder and pedals then you will need to steer as for any other kayak using the paddle strokes themselves.

Sea kayaks come in a number of flavours including 'sit on' for quick jaunts in relatively flat water, and 'sit in' where you have a moulded bucket seat below the level of the deck. In difficult conditions the sit in versions may also have a full rubberised spray deck which goes around your waist (like a kilt for perverts) and clips onto the kayak. Two-man kayaks make the most efficient use of energy, though a bit like waterborne tandems they can also lead to spectacular domestic rows about who is doing the paddling/how well you steer, whatever. Bear in mind that in two-person canoes without rudders it is generally the person at the back who does the steering (while the person in front paddles for dear life), while those equipped with pedals often have them so that the front paddler steers.

If paddling kayaks floats your boat then maybe it's time to look at white-water kayaking in IDEA 42, *Wild-water and white-water slalom*.

Try another idea...

Remember that while there are kayaks designed for flirting with breaking waves (often with a curious flared bow a little like a mini-aircraft carrier) most sea kayaks are not designed to deal with surf, so don't be tempted to follow the surf 'slippers' into the breakers. If you have to launch and land through mild surf then aim straight into it and push on through it as fast as you can.

'The winds and the waves are always on the side of the ablest navigators.'
EDWARD GIBBON (British historian, 1737–1794)

Defining idea...

Q I'm keen to have a go using a collapsible kayak but have been warned about performance shortfalls – is this a problem?

A *Frankly, no, not unless you're racing. Modern collapsibles use a tight skin stretched over a skeleton frame and the results are nearly as stable as their hard-bodied brothers. You wouldn't want to play near rocks or surf if you could avoid it, though.*

Q I really enjoy the idea of kayaking all day but get really tired – any thoughts?

A *You can either improve your efficiency (see 'Here's an idea for you'), your muscular endurance (lots of time on the rowing machine) or you could look into the possibility of using small kayak sails. These are common in expedition kayaking and can be stowed when not in use. For obvious reasons they won't help you all the time, but unless 100% of your paddling is upwind they will certainly save some sweat over a long day.*

45

Windsurfing

Take the pure pleasure of harnessing the wind for power, add a bucketful of surfing chic, a bit of freestyle cool borrowed from skateboarding and you have windsurfing.

Truly the most liberating way to sail...

Windsurfing kit has come a long way since the board I first tried my hand on twenty years ago. I don't know what they fed sailboards on back then but those beasties were big, heavy and mean. I remember spending pretty much an entire day falling off into the water and clumsily climbing back out again. Just to break up the routine a little I would occasionally indulge in brief, clammy, full-contact bouts with the sail before going in off the other side. Should anyone ever want to recreate the lost pleasures of learning old-style windsurfing they could get a reasonable approximation by grappling with a wet sheet while balancing on an ironing board. If they ever invent a sport that involves wrestling the entire contents of a Kowloon laundry I will be uniquely well-qualified to take on all comers.

These days modern composite materials, plus the use of bracing in the sail itself, has resulted in light, taut, much easier to handle rigs and with it a much more enjoyable learning curve for the beginner and a world of possibilities for the master.

Modern boards essentially come in two different types. Long boards tend to be aimed at beginners with a lot of stability and buoyancy to help balance. Typically they will also have a dagger board – a centreline rudder that slots through the

Here's an idea for you...

No doubt about it, if you want to look the part then the beach start is where it's at. Start in knee-deep water with the nose of your board pointed straight out into the waves. Raise the rig and stand close to the board, slightly behind it rather than front on, looking across it. Remember that if you step up with one foot onto the tail of the board it will sink and the board will spin, so balance that by lifting the rig forwards, extending the front arm while at the same time 'sheeting in' with the back. This should create a twisting force which helps counterbalance your body as you simultaneously step up onto the board, front foot near the mast base and resisting the lift of the nose by pushing the board flat.

board and enables you to sail much closer to the wind. Sails come in different sizes too and the smaller the sail the easier it is to handle, so make sure you start out with the biggest board teamed up with the smallest sail available.

Short boards are better suited for choppier water and greater wind strength. Their characteristics have been pushed to the point where the highest performance boards now are only just neutrally buoyant, meaning that they require 'planing winds' (force 3 or 4 and above) in order to sail and rise above the water's surface. Typically a short board will not have a dagger board – which makes them much more manoeuvrable, but also harder to master. They will also have foot straps which, in conjunction with a harness, allow the better sailors to control boards even in quite extreme moves. Short boards essentially come in three types, defined by the three main disciplines of performance sailing.

- Slalom boards are the commonest boards and the chances are that those are what those cool-looking individuals are using as they carve curves into the waves when gybing (turning through the wind with the wind behind them).

- Free ride boards are the stunt boards – sort of a mutant hybrid between sailing and skateboarding that has yacht club commodores reaching for their pink gins. Freestyle windsurfing includes spins, pirouettes and skateboard moves and since it doesn't require any particular form of wave it is often practised on inland waters.

- Wave boards: wave sailing is somewhere in between freestyle and surfing. The aim is to ride the face of big waves for as long as possible, just off the breaking point, before cutting up the wave face and jumping as high up into the air as possible. While they're up there wave sailors will usually while away the time with 360° degree turns, spins and anything else they can dream up.

If windsurfing thrills you, imagine what it would be like to fly across waves at much higher speeds and in much higher winds. How? By switching from a sail to a kite – take a look at kite surfing in IDEA 28, *Catching air – kite surfing*.

Try another idea...

'You can't stop the waves, but you can learn to surf.'
JON KABAT-ZINN, meditation teacher

Defining idea...

197

How did it go?

Q   I can't even stand up on the damn thing, how is this ever going to work?

A   *That sounds familiar. Try finding a surf school with a simulator – essentially a windsurfing rig mounted on a pivot on land. That way you can get used to the basics of stance and foot positioning without all that tiresome falling in and climbing back out again.*

Q   I'm up but I just don't have the arm strength to lift the rig out of the water, what am I doing wrong?

A   *Relying on your arms, by the sound of it. Position yourself securely on the centreline of the board with your feet at right angles to the nose/tail and your body squatting low on your thighs. Now tuck your butt in and lean back to use your own body weight and the strength of your legs to haul the rig out of the water. Start to stand as the rig lifts and pull the rig up towards the nose/tail rather than straight up towards the middle. Slide the rig clear of the water in a curving movement rather than jerking it up.*

46

Get the in-lines on

In-line skating is smooth, fluid and fun. It's easy to get into, as hard as you like to get really good at and can be the starting point for fitness, street style or flat-out speed training.

Of course it's also one of the fastest ways of bringing arse and earth together. Practice makes perfect.

In-line skating goes back to attempts to continue the ice skating season. Arguably the first attempt to sell in-line skates commercially was the 'Rolito' offered by Robert John Tyers of London in 1823. In 1980 Scott and Brennan Olson of Minneapolis, both ice-hockey players, decided to bring the in-line skate up to date. By mating a hockey boot with polyurethane wheels and a rubber heel brake they created what is identifiably the modern in-line skate and started off a company, Rollerblade, in the process. Now the word 'rollerblade' and the term in-line skating are synonymous.

The problem with in-line skating ('blading' if you prefer) is that it also became synonymous with the smug self-satisfaction of the 80s. Close your eyes and you can

Here's an idea for you...

There's a classic plateau in blading where you are comfortable enough with basic stopping and turning and so don't really try to learn anything more complex. Classically this is when you've mastered the heel brake but aren't yet slide stopping or T-stopping. Sounds like you? Choose a safe place, take the Allen keys with you and remove that heel brake altogether. Now you'll have to experiment with different techniques for stopping. You'll also find it much easier to try step-overs and heel to toe moves without a brake you can catch on the ground. Replace the heel brake when taking to the road unless you are 100% sure of your new-found skills or you may end up munching macadam.

summon up loads of media images of cheesy types sweeping gracefully along beachfronts. Some extreme sports followers have also snubbed in-line skating for being too easy to get into – not sufficiently niche. But that is precisely what is so great about it. In-line skating can be whatever you want it to be. It's a great low-impact fitness activity – which was what its creators had in mind – and a means of transport to rival the bicycle. In its 'aggressive' or 'street' form it rivals anything skateboarders can manage, and in flat-out speed it is now appearing alongside traditional foot races across the world. You probably first came across it as a distraction for an hour or two in a park. Now think about where you can go with it.

AGGRESSIVE

Street-style skating is a close brother to skateboarding and initially provoked rivalries and clashes at half-pipes and vert ramps. Street skates have small wheels protected at the sides by metal sheets to enable better 'grinding' moves down handrails and ramps. Some skaters even remove the middle wheels to get a bigger and better 'grind' surface. A combination of improved blades and improved bladers means that the skateboarders no longer hold the high ground in urban skating and are just as likely to be seen learning from the bladers' moves.

Enjoy wheel sports but want to go faster? Try IDEA 49, *Land yachting*.

Try another idea...

HOCKEY

If you've mastered stops, turns and sudden acceleration and are looking for a new challenge then roller hockey is for you. Essentially it's ice hockey on wheels – only with the advantages that you don't need dedicated ice rinks (a car park will do) and there's rather less physical violence.

SPEED

Long, low and mean, the speed skates are immediately recognisable by their five (rather than the normal four) wheels and low, ankle-high leather boot. Of course it's also a bit of a giveaway that the people wearing them are often sheathed in Lycra and crouching so low you'd think they were indulging in an unusually high-speed search for a lost contact lens. Roller marathons are now common and take place alongside high-profile sporting events such as the Berlin Marathon.

'Unlike skateboarding the rewards of rollerblading are immediate and consistent. The process of learning to skate on in-lines is constantly gratifying so participants are encouraged to stick with it.'
ARLO EISENBERG, X Games gold medallist in aggressive skating. Remember that as you pick yourself up off the tarmac. Again.

Defining idea...

SOCIAL

Many of the world's big cities now have weekly outings where hundreds of in-line skaters get together to flirt, compare notes, amuse the kids or simply irritate car drivers. In Paris they even close the roads to traffic and provide a rollerblading posse of police riding shotgun. Rest breaks are common and the atmosphere is carnival. Give it a go.

DOWNHILL

Oh yes they do. There are downhill races on in-line skates with everything that entails in terms of streamlined helmets, grimly set jaws and spectacular roadrash. Brakes? They only slow you down.

The fact that rollerblading is relatively easy to learn (honest, stick with it) makes it accessible to a large number of people and helps create a slightly more democratic feel with less sense of tribalism than skateboarding. Don't presume that this means tribes don't exist, however. When I first took lessons (highly recommended) I remember our instructor watching speed skaters doing laps before snorting 'speed skaters, hah – some of those guys can't even skate backwards.' 'Hah' we all echoed dismissively, clinging desperately to each other in an attempt to stay upright. Don't be put off by this, just get stuck in and have fun.

Q   **My main way of stopping is to heel brake, but it doesn't seem to be enough – why?**

How did it go?

A   *It could be that you're barrelling downhill beyond your abilities but it's most likely that you're not being bold enough in extending your braking foot forwards. Bend your non-braking leg further and extend the braking heel out further forwards in the 'whoops, I've slipped on a banana skin' posture to get better 'bite' from the brake.*

Q   **Blading is great but I live in Britain and it gets wet. Any tips on staying upright?**

A   *Emigrating? OK, bigger moves mean less control as your blades come to the end of the push, so increase your cadence and reduce the sweep of each stroke so that you have less power but more control with each stroke. It may seem a little like mincing on wheels, but it beats falling over.*

47

Simply scuba

Immersed in an alien element, breathing and movement slowed, weightless as an astronaut – scuba diving offers a unique chance to explore the 'inner space' that covers seven-tenths of the planet.

It is simply magical... and means many things to many people.

A steady diet of Jacques Cousteau since the 60s has led many people to associate scuba with rainbows of reef fishes, razor-toothed sharks and encounters with whales. For some, the sole purpose of the seabed is to provide a home for the remains of wrecked ships. Another group will talk endlessly about the dangers of the deep and the thrills of diving down to the limits of safety. A rare few will smile contentedly and talk of the simple pleasure of just being and breathing underwater without the need to surface for an hour or so. The oceans are large enough to accommodate them all.

One popular misconception is that it takes ages to get the necessary qualifications to go diving. That used to be the case, and certainly when I started diving through the old club system it was months before we were even allowed to put a dainty neoprene-clad toe into the water. Now, however, all of the major diving organisations have wised up to the fact that people want to enjoy themselves right here and right now. Diving qualifications get as complex as you can wish, but the

Here's an idea for you...

Try nitrox diving. To extend the limits of bottom time and depth it is possible to use a number of enriched breathing mixtures which change the levels of the major gasses. Nitrox is a mixture where oxygen and nitrogen dominate – which means that technically normal air is nitrox (air is roughly 21% oxygen, 78% nitrogen). For the purposes of diving, however, nitrox normally refers to mixes where the oxygen levels have been increased, the advantage of which is longer dives with shorter surface intervals. You need to qualify, but the joy of a nitrox course is that it's a brief theory course – once underwater you just get on with breathing so it can be a great qualification to get prior to diving wrecks, for example, lying at a depth that normally permits only a few minutes at the bottom.

major organisations all offer a very basic entry point where you can go diving (under supervision) right away to see if you like it. As can the kids – even those as young as ten. After that it's just a question of taking it as far as you wish. Here are a few ideas of where you might want to go with it.

MARINE CONSERVATION

Many organisations now use volunteer divers to help with the work of charting marine life as part of measuring our impact on the oceans and how to preserve them. Sometimes referred to as 'starfish counting' this can be a great way to put a little back. You may also want to take part in 'clean-up dives' where volunteers help to tidy up the daily debris that finds its way into the sea.

MARINE ARCHAEOLOGY

As above, it is becoming increasingly common for volunteer divers to join the ranks of foot-soldiers marking and mapping wrecks, prehistoric fish traps and sunken cities.

Normally this involves a brief introductory course in archaeology before working under the supervision of qualified archaeologists. At its best it may mean you get to dive on sites that have previously been reserved for a privileged few from the scientific community.

Fancy taking your scuba expertise further? Check out IDEA 3, *Solid sky*, on ice diving or IDEA 8, *Cave diving* – or even freediving at IDEA 25, *The big blue*.

Try another idea...

WRECK DIVING

Where there are wrecks there are usually reputable dive centres (look for membership of organisations such as PADI, NAUI, BSAC or CMAS) offering wreck-diving specialty courses. Not only will this give you specific information on the wrecks but it can prepare you for the skills needed to penetrate wrecks where safe to do so.

TECH (TECHNICAL) DIVING

By mixing different gasses into the cocktail (commonly 'tri-mix' which blends nitrogen, oxygen and helium) it becomes possible to go deeper for longer and therefore access sites beyond the reach of most divers. Tech diving is also associated with sinister black clothing, plus lots of impressive metal D-rings and gadgets, all of which make you suspect that, in fashion terms at least, it never made it out of the 8os.

'The best way to observe fish is to become a fish. And the best way to become a fish – or a reasonable facsimile thereof – is to don an underwater breathing device called the aqualung.'
JACQUES-YVES COUSTEAU

Defining idea...

Q **A friend of mine told me that if I wanted to dive I have to do the PADI test and that takes a week. Is that right?**

A *Common mixup. PADI isn't a test or a qualification, it's the Professional Association of Dive Instructors and the leading provider of training and qualifications so there are many different PADI qualifications. PADI, in line with the other major organisations (NAUI, CMAS, BSAC, etc.,) now offers qualifications at pretty much every level including 'discovery' packages that get you in the water the morning you rock up.*

Q **I tried diving when I was younger – it mainly involved miserable sessions shivering in and out of a bleak flooded quarry. Why would I go back?**

A *You too, huh? Why did we do that? These days cheap travel and the growth of the recreational dive industry mean you can jet off to the Red Sea or Thailand and be exploring coral reefs in gin-clear water and swimming-pool temperatures. Leave your old, cold impressions behind.*

Q **I had a panic attack on a boat dive and haven't been back in the water since. Any ideas?**

A *Boat dives can be stressful. Take away some of the stressors and try again, so dive with a friend rather than strangers and insist on diving off a gently sloping beach so you have an easy entry and exit. If you were cold then get advice on better protection (a hood, perhaps) to take that element out of the picture. Eliminate the things you didn't like one at a time and suddenly you'll find yourself enjoying the underwater realm as it is meant to be.*

48

World Wide Weird

Bog snorkelling, wife carrying, Zorbing; this idea looks at the loonier limits of adventure sports. One person's extreme is another's mainstream, and the quest for adventure sports around the globe has led to some activities that suggest that any participating 'athletes' would have to be insane. Here is a selection...

'There's nowt so queer as folk' goes a saying in the North of England — not a reflection on their sexual tastes (or so I am assured), more an acknowledgment that whatever weirdness your tastes may run to, there's always someone else prepared to go one better.

While the majority of extreme sports seem to have originated in the Southern Hemisphere it takes Northern Europeans to come up with the really loopy end of the scale. The following don't so much 'push the envelope' as burst right through it and keep going without looking back.

211

Here's an idea for you... **Stay at home, watch TV, read a nice book. You know it makes more sense than any of the above. Of course if you absolutely must have a go at this sort of thing then you can find a festival of absurd sports in most corners of the globe from online festival guides. Try www.gorp.com and click on the 'worldwide festivals' section.**

WIFE CARRYING - FINLAND

Nordic peoples still clearly look back nostalgically on a time when hats with cow horns were the height of fashion and the gentle art of courtship consisted largely of seizing the object of your desire and hurling her over your shoulder before legging it off back to the longboat. Times have changed, of course, and the hats are but a distant memory. Running around with someone else's wife over your shoulder, however, is still very much alive and kicking as a concept, and indeed as a contest.

At the annual wife-carrying championships in Sonkajarvi, Finland, wives must weigh at least 49 kg and be carried over a sand and grass course of 253.5 m including two 'dry obstacles' and a 'water obstacle' about a metre deep. You mustn't drop the wife and you must have fun (you must, it's specifically mentioned in the rules). You'd be surprised at the size of some of the wives people opt to carry, which might seem a touching tribute to true love, until you find out that the prize for the carrier is the wife's weight in beer. There's more at www.sonkajarvi.fi – look for the link 'wife carrying' in English.

FIERLJEPPEN - THE NETHERLANDS

They have a lot of canals in Holland, and seemingly a lot of spare time on their hands – how else do you explain a sporting ritual in which people of all ages aim to pole vault their way across canals? Every August they come together to display their prowess. A pole (polsstok) is planted firmly in the middle of the canal, and the aim is to sprint at it from one bank, jump to it, climb to the top and try to control its overbalancing so you land firmly on your feet on the other side

Appreciate a ration of humour with your adventure? Try IDEA 40, *Extreme ironing – ironing in the soul.*

Try another idea...

of the canal. Well, that's the idea. In practice there's a predictable list of potential disasters including missing the pole, slipping down it, not climbing high enough or overbalancing it in the wrong direction. All of which can only have one result for the athlete. More from www.pbholland.com.

BOG SNORKELLING – WALES

Only the British could have gazed upon the stinking, soggy slime of a Welsh peat bog and instantly been inspired with the desire to plunge in and make it a sporting venue. At Llanwrtyd Wells competitors don snorkels, fins and wet suits (optional), then fin like the clappers from one end of a 60 m trench to the other and back. The water is deep brown and filthy. Visibility is zero. As I say, only the British.

BOG CYCLING – WALES

Or maybe that should be only the Welsh – they took bog snorkelling one step further, also at Llanwrtyd Wells. Why waste a good bog, after all? In bog cycling the competitors have to cycle two lengths of a trench cut in the bog, riding specially prepared mountain bikes with lead-

'The wife to be carried may be your own, the neighbour's or you may have found her farther afield; she must, however, be over seventeen years of age.'
Official rules, Finnish wife-carrying competition

Defining idea...

filled tyres. Again a wet suit is 'recommended'. As is a nice lie-down in a darkened room should the idea ever appeal. You can find more on both bog snorkelling and bog cycling at http://llanwrtyd-wells.powys.org.uk.

ZORBING – NEW ZEALAND

OK, so this is a Southern Hemisphere invention, but according to the Dangerous Sports Club of Oxford (the people who came up with modern bungee jumping) the original idea was Welsh, so really it's just confirmation of the above. A Zorb is pretty much an oversize beach ball you can ride in. You're strapped into it and pushed down a hill whilst trying very hard to control your bodily functions since anything released into the Zorb is going to continue to slosh around until you come to a halt. There is a variation called the Wet Zorb, which was presumably inspired by what happens when a personal accident occurs in a dry Zorb. In the Wet Zorb you aren't strapped in but instead encouraged to try and stay upright like a huge two-legged hamster in a wheel. Just to make sure you can't actually do this the friendly Zorbmeisters throw some warm soapy water in there with you to keep you company. If you thought the hamster image was undignified you're not going to feel overly clever as you slosh your way down the hill like a boozed-up jogger caught in the spin cycle.

How did it go?

Q   I got soaked, battered and bruised, what am I doing wrong?

A   *You're taking part, that's what you're doing. What were you thinking?*

Q   Do I get to keep the wife?

A   *Depends on how far you can run with her, I suppose. And whether anyone's chasing. What the hell, give it a go.*

49

Land yachting

'Three wheels, no brakes and God's foot on the accelerator!'

Land yachting is fast, furious and oddly silent — like a drag race with the volume set to 'mute'.

Although the terms 'yacht' and 'land sailor' suggest a strong relationship with sailing and the sea, the reality of land yachts is that they have more in common with high speed go-carts than they do with anything you might see gliding across the water. Modern land yachts are breathtakingly fast (reaching speeds in excess of 120 km/h), with the kind of acceleration that pins your internal organs to your backbone and spin-on-a-penny handling. They're a far cry from the lumpen, windmill on wheels contraptions that Louis Blériot (yes, the original cross channel flyer) sailed along the beaches of Hardelot in France a hundred years ago. Modern yachts use an aerodynamic wing and have fuselages made of light-weight, high-strength composites (although the axles are usually good old ash wood).

There are two main classes of land yacht raced, class 3 and class 5, both of which involve sitting down on a three-wheeled chassis with a single sail like a gull's wing soaring above you. Of these class 3 are the fastest things around but the similar looking class 5 are the most popular since they can more easily be dismantled and

Here's an idea for you...

You don't have to learn to sail to enjoy land sailing. A couple of years ago a Kiwi invention called the Blokart was exported to the world and brought a whole new dimension to the idea of land yachting. The Blokart is clearly the result of a night of passion between a land yacht and a go-cart. They're small, light and steered with a steering wheel. They can hit speeds of up to 90 km/h but stop just by swerving so that they face into the wind. Traditional land sailors may sneer but for the rest of us Blokarts mean we don't have to learn how to sail, and we don't need miles of beach or desert to get going in. If you have a space the size of a tennis court available then you can just get in, belt up and blast. Try www.blokart.com for details of blokarting near you.

carried on a car roof rack. In terms of sailing the fact that you only have one sail to operate means that it is more like windsurfing from a near-horizontal position than dinghy sailing. Windsurfers, incidentally, will be delighted to learn that class 7 is dedicated to what is known as a speedsailor – instantly recognisable as a windsurfing board on wheels. Class 8 is designated for new craft including paracarts – basically kite surfing meets land sailing in which the pilot/sailor uses a large kite for power and a wheeled chassis to stand on. The sport is constantly evolving.

As well as a land yacht you also need plenty of space to sail in. Beaches and airfields are the most popular in Europe (including the beaches of the Opal Coast where Blériot pioneered the sport), while the semi-deserts of Australia and the US provide even larger venues. Sailing can be done in a wide range of conditions but a steady wind is infinitely safer than gusty weather, not least because the land yacht's capacity for acceleration can make for a more hair-raising ride than you anticipated if the wind gods decide to play with you and your toy.

You don't need a licence to have a go, and most clubs will be more than happy to introduce newcomers to the sport, but it will take a few sessions under expert supervision before you are truly going to be up and running. An understanding of sailing, of tacking and gybing, as well as the limits of the chassis and the protocol of piloting near others will all need to be grasped before you can spread your wing sail. Don't be put off, though, since the existence of mini yachts, intended to be piloted by kids and packed in a car boot, should give you some idea of the availability of the sport to anyone who wants to give it a go.

There are so many ways to go if land sailing appeals and they don't have to involve traditional sailing (though you'll find that in IDEA 23, *Messing about in boats*). If you want to learn to harness the wind and fly across the waves at ludicrous speeds and in all weathers then you should turn straight to IDEA 28, *Catching air*, and find out about kite surfing.

Try another idea...

'"God": The word that comes after "go-cart".'
SAMUEL BUTLER (English novelist, essayist and critic). Not only correct in a dictionary sense, but in what you're likely to end up saying at the helm of a land yacht

Defining idea...

Q   I have never sailed in my life so how can I handle even something simple like a Blokart?

A   *You really don't need to understand sailing to Blokart – that's one of the things traditional land sailors hate about it. Even a complete beginner can get going by first establishing the wind direction (just throw some grass in the air) and then set off at a right angle to it. At the end of your run, turn back and come back the way you came.*

Q   So can I use these things as transport?

A   *Not unless you live in a very large, flat area with no roads. Blokarts may have simplified land sailing but they still can't sail directly into the wind. Going upwind means tacking (zigzagging across the face of the wind) and that might prove a little risky on the public highway.*

Sk8 – skateboarding for dudes, dudettes and duds

For those of us who live on a street, rather than by the ocean, sand dunes or snow-capped mountains, skateboarding is often the only board sport available.

It's cheap, it's fun and no, you're never too old to start.

I remember the 70s skateboard craze like it was yesterday. City councils held fervent debates about whether sinking a few half-pipes into the car parks would get kids off drugs, and indignant pimply people grumbled on TV about why skateboarding wasn't an Olympic sport when synchronised swimming was (still a fairly compelling argument, I find). Best of all, parents tutted and shook their heads in a deeply satisfying way at the mere mention of Big Red wheels and Silver Fox trucks. It was heaven. Or at least it would have been if I could have boarded. Sadly, even then, my God-given talent for falling off things was proving a problem for my playground cred and so skateboarding rather passed me by.

I barely glanced at a skateboard for another twenty or so years, and then all of a sudden people of my age were at it again – this time with what seemed like

Here's an idea for you...

It doesn't matter if you're a complete newcomer or returning to the board after a long absence, the 'ollie' is a simple trick to make it look like you could be pulling huge jumps off a vert ramp if only you had a mind to. It's also the basic building block for most of the tricks you will pull on a vert ramp should you get that good. Get up a little speed and keep your front foot on the middle of the board with your back foot on the tail. Push down with your back foot (bringing up the nose of the board), and slide your front foot towards the nose as you jump up pulling your knees into your chest – the board should rise with you. Follow the board back down to a safe landing. Look suitably rad.

surfboards on wheels, I grant you, but unmistakeably skateboards nonetheless. Now you see longboards, skinny little short boards, you name it. I notice the trend for tiny wheels seems to have passed but you just know it'll come back again.

Skateboarding is cheap and simple, anybody can propel themselves along and you don't have to have a skate park, a half-pipe or a ramp in order to get going and learn tricks. Just hop on. Of course in doing so you will define yourself as:

- Regular – 'normal' stance with left foot forwards.
- Goofy – the reverse, for those who normally favour the left foot and so have the right foot at the front.
- Switch – a goofy rider who rides regular, a regular guy who goofs just to see.
- Mongo – mongo-footed means that you're pushing the board along with the forward foot – not normally an efficient way of getting about.
- Fakie. Fakie means you're riding backwards. NB: this is only considered cool if it is done deliberately.

Having got on the board you now have to decide just what kind of skating you intend to do.

If you like board riding but fancy getting away from the tarmac then why not try skateboarding on the dunes: sandboarding – see IDEA 31, *Circles in the sand.*

Try another idea...

- Slalom – weaving in and out of those old drinks cans. Empty ones are less painful when you crash into them and fall off.
- Downhill – are you mad?
- Freestyle – tricktastic. Besides after just half a day of trying to flip your board and pull 360s your abs will get a better workout than from any number of crunches.
- Vertical – shooting up and down ramps, just like on TV only with rather more falling over.
- To the shops – not the pinnacle of artistry perhaps, but one of the all-time great boarding opportunities nonetheless.
- Pool – empty swimming pools attract skaters like flies to honey. Of course this is more useful to know if you live in Malibu rather than Manchester, but still.

One little word of advice here. I realise that they are profoundly uncool, but knee/elbow protections and a helmet will undoubtedly save you an awful lot of damage if you are new to skateboarding or returning from a long absence. You're going to get laughed at by teenagers anyway, so what difference does it make?

'So why is it, if you're forty and snowboard you're classed as cool but forty on a skateboard and apparently you should know better?'
CARL ARNFIELD, chrome-dome mastermind behind www.middle-age-shred.com

Defining idea...

How did it go?

Q **Terrible. I try to do the ollie but the board and I part company mid-air and I either land with one foot on and one foot off or I miss it altogether. Why?**

A *Take a look at what your shoulders are up to while you're trying to land. In board sports shoulders pretty much always determine direction, and in an ollie if your shoulders don't line up with the board as you land then your feet won't land on it.*

Q **I am barely leaving the ground, what am I doing wrong?**

A *Well, you might simply not be jumping high enough, or you may think you're jumping because you're lifting your front foot but you're actually pushing down in the air with your back foot and so keeping the board low. Focus on a two-footed jump and landing.*

Q **Nope, still having trouble, and getting tired at being laughed at by the local kids. Any ideas before I bin the board and go back to accountancy?**

A *Ollieblocks. Ollieblocks are hard plastic replacements for wheels so you can practice ollies and all in the safety and intimacy of your own home without the board or yourself going anywhere.*

Xterra Xcitement

Triathlon can be a great way of working out without overdoing it on any one discipline. Or it can be a flat-out flurry of feet and pedals against the clock – introducing triathlon for people who don't 'do' roads.

Either way taking it off-road adds a whole new dimension — whether you're mainly interested in mastering the scenery with your technical skills, or just looking at it as you go by.

Getting my kit ready for my very first triathlon I found myself parked alongside a team of professional triathletes. They were wheeling greyhound-sleek, carbon fibre racing bikes out of the back of a van and stopped to watch as I grunted and heaved my rusty mountain bike out of the boot of the car. One stepped forward, looked hard at my soviet-tractor-style steed, gave a low whistle and pronounced me 'hardcore'. Even as I came in stone cold last in that race we both knew that I had the moral advantage. Somehow road bikes, however swift and graceful, will always be that little bit prissy, while mud-spattered, knobbly-tyred, mountain bikes are the

Here's an idea for you... **Quite fancy the idea of off-road tri but not sure you're up to it? Then break it down and try it for yourself. If you are a member of a gym you may be able to swim, then move to cycling and running machines to complete the distance. If you're doing it outside of a gym then consider the swimming as a separate event but focus on cycling and then going straight into the run (called a 'brick' by the pros) – it'll help you get used to the jelly legs feeling as your legs, already tired from cycling, are now expected to carry on working but this time with the weight of your body on them.**

proud badges of a breed of mud-spattered, knobbly sort of person. On the knobbly basis alone Xterra and I were made for each other.

Triathlon has been one of the great growth sports of the last twenty years because anyone who can swim and cycle and run can have a go. Once the preserve of elite athletes it has now proved popular amongst the rest of us who paddle, peddle and plod our way to the finish. What Xterra brings to that combination is large amounts of dirt and the chance to get your outside as muddy, mucky and messy as your inner child is already.

An event doesn't have to be Xterra to be an off-road triathlon, and some purists sneer at Xterra for its commerciality (you'll find there's an Xterra branded trail shoe, watch, car and entire clothing line). On the other hand the Xterra brand has gone a long way to getting sponsorship and organising a worldwide series so it's the one you'll most likely come across. It all kicked off in 1996 in an event called Aquaterra in Maui, thereby adhering to the rule that all good adventure sports start off somewhere implausibly exotic and end up in a muddy pit somewhere near you. Aquaterra took the standard triathlon format and beat it out of shape a little until it consisted of an open ocean swim, a mountain bike race and a trail run. That's basically what you've got to this day, with the distances typically being a 1.5 km open-water swim, followed by a 30 km mountain bike ride and a 10 km trail run. In order to make it even more open to the rest of us, a 'sprint' distance – called Xterra Sport – offers newcomers an introductory distance of a 500 m swim, a 15 km mountain bike ride and a 5 km trail run.

Xterra now claims to be the fastest-growing multi-sport event across the world and it's not difficult to see why. Take the appeal of the outdoors, throw in unpredictable courses that can have even the experts getting off their bikes to push, and you have a levelling sport that feels less elitist, and which is often in beautiful surroundings. Besides, while not many of us have a quality road-racing bike around the place there are precious few that can't get their hands on a beaten-up mountain bike.

If this all sounds too much for you, why not have a go at Idea 30, *Triple fun – triathlon*.

try another idea...

'*The mountain bikers brought their laid-back style and bold self-assurance. The triathletes brought their hardcore training and avid dedication.*'
From the Xterra official website, shamefully forgetting to mention that the rest of us mainly brought sandwiches and sticking plasters

Defining idea...

How did it go?

Q **A mate has offered me a diving wetsuit for the swim – good or bad idea?**

A *Diving wetsuits rarely have the flexibility in the arms that swimming wetsuits do – try to get a swimming or surfing suit if you can. If you have no other option and the water is going to be chilly then try out the suit before the race; remember the golden rule that everything in a race is tried and tested, nothing is new.*

Q **I can swim, cycle and run. My problem is transition, where I wrestle with my wetsuit, struggle with swimming costume and settle the issue of shoes and socks by three falls and a submission. Any clues?**

A *Transition is sometimes called the fourth discipline of triathlon. Keep it smooth by practising beforehand and keeping changes to a minimum. Don't take a swimming costume – instead swim in your Lycra running/cycling shorts and shirt. Don't worry about the fact that they'll be wet; you won't notice after a few minutes on the bike. Use a lubricant on the wrists and neck of your wetsuit – make sure it's not petroleum based, as that rots rubber, but something like cocoa butter will help you slip out of the suit (and smell acceptable too). Some people train without socks so that they can do without them altogether on race day.*

52

Going ultra – beyond the marathon

Time was when it was thought that the marathon was reserved for extraordinary athletes. Now, with a bit of dedication, the next door neighbour can manage it. In a rhino costume.

So if you're already a marathoner, why not go all the way and set your sights on an ultrathon?

Technically any race longer than the 42.2 km of a marathon can be billed as an 'ultrathon', but while you'd think that would lead to a rash of races at 42.3 km (just to sex up the T-shirts if nothing else) there is a wide range of distances from 50 km to 555 km. Each has their own challenges, and therefore each brings their own flavour of achievement and self-satisfaction but always with the knowledge that as an endurance athlete you're pushing yourself just a bit further than even the marathoners. The major differences between these races revolve around certain factors.

ON-ROAD RACES

Pounding tarmac is much harder on the body (you'll be easing yourself downstairs backwards for a couple of days), but much more likely to be accessible to spectators and have regular support stations. The world's largest ultra in terms of numbers is South

Here's an idea for you...

If you're coming from normal road racing/jogging and you're not sure about how to start in ultras then don't throw yourself in at the deep end with a multi-day self-sufficiency race. Instead pick a single day event and aim for an off-road race which majors on rolling and rugged scenery. Now make a pre-race resolution to walk the hills. All the hills. Use your hands on your thighs to help push on the really steep stuff. You'll be surprised how competitive you will be if you can keep up a brisk walking pace, and because you will vary your pace so much you are much less likely to end up thrashing around at the limits of your abilities than you would racing a flat race.

Africa's Comrades 'Marathon' which alternates each year from Durban to Pietermaritzburg (uphill run) or the reverse (downhill) and sees 12,000 runners (most ultras muster a field of thirty to a hundred runners) aim to cover the 87 km course before the 12-hour cut-off. Pretty much the whole nation seems to turn out to cheer them on. Other major on-road races include the annual 100 km championships at Millau in France and the legendary Badwater along the roads of Death Valley. By contrast there are minor (but nonetheless curiously poignant) local runs such as the Adak 100 in Swedish Lapland in which you run through the night by the light of the midnight sun. All very scenic – at least until the point where you frankly stop caring about scenery and just wish for it all to be over.

OFF-ROAD RACES

Scenery is part and parcel of off-road ultras because you're running through it rather than looking at it. Off-road ultras have more in common with trail running than they do with marathons and vary widely as different parts of the world tend to play up local strengths. Mountainous countries offer 'sky races' (whether in Swaziland or the Alps) which will have you charging up the steeper bits of scenery (and wheezing back down again), while desert races have developed as a genre in their own right, and can be found in the Kalahari (Augrabies

Extreme), Sahara (Marathon des Sables) and the Gobi (Gobi March) amongst others.

Like the idea, but fancy something a bit different? Check out extreme adventure racing at IDEA 11, *This is a raid!*

Try another idea...

STAGE RACES

Stage races break the route up into chunks to be taken on each day. So, for example, such epics as the Marathon des Sables and Augrabies Extreme work on a model of a 250 km race across the desert, but spread over six days of running (and a rest day).

NON-STOP RACES

A non-stop race doesn't mean that *you* must keeping going without stopping, but more that the clock doesn't stop. For example, the Trans 333 and Trans 555 (333 km and 555 km respectively across West Africa) leave it down to the individual when and where they stop and for how long – but every power nap or cigarette break will add to their time.

SUPPORTED OR SELF-SUFFICIENT RACES

In a self-sufficient race you will be asked to carry all your kit – food, bedding, cooking implements, safety items, trouser press, whatever – with you as you run. Only water is supplied en route. Supported races mean that you're not carrying a rucksack but are fed, watered and generally nurtured as you go by a support team. Some long-distance supported races are effectively high-speed self-propelled tourism with routes taking you through the Dogon country in Mali or along the Great Wall of China with accommodation laid on each night. There's one ultra in Britain which is a

> '*All men should strive to learn before they die, what they are running from, and to, and why.*'
> JAMES THURBER (1894–1961)
> American writer and humorist

Defining idea...

cunningly disguised bed-and-breakfast holiday across the country or, if you prefer, a giant pub crawl but spread out over a greater distance than usual. Larger supported races generally aim to cater for all levels of running (and walking/hobbling/staggering) abilities so there's something for pretty much everyone who fancies tugging on their trainers and taking to the great outdoors in the search for the ultra.

How did it go?

Q **I'm interested in a self-sufficient stage race in an exotic location but there seems so much to think about (what food? what clothes?) so how can I find out how to prepare and whether it's within my abilities?**

A *Simple – if it's a big and famous race then the Web is probably awash with race reports about it (try www.eventrate.com for a start). If it's not, then contact the organisers and ask to be put in touch with one or more previous contestants to ask them for tips and advice. You'll find most people will fall over themselves to talk about these events and the preparation they put into them. Trust me, I barely shut up about it.*

Q **Aside from 'all over' which bits of me are likely to suffer most and how can I avoid that?**

A *Good training will help protect your muscles, good shoes will help cosset your joints so get expert advice on both from someone who knows the specific race (see above). The other area that hurts, however, is usually your feet: specifically blisters. Invest in a proper pair of 'twin-skinned' socks, an industrial-sized tub of anti-chafe (slap it on all over) and if you don't know about wrapping your toes then find someone who does to explain the dark arts of taping tootsies.*

The end...

Or is it a new beginning? We hope that you've been inspired to have a go at something new. Remember we said, 'if you're not living on the edge you're taking up too much space', and that it's up to you to work out where the edge is? Well, it still is. Let us know what you saw when you peeked over the edge. We'd love to share the excitement.

If there was an idea that you struggled to understand, tell us about that too. Tell us how you got on generally. What did it for you – what helped you to fight the panic and take the plunge? Maybe you've got some tips of your own that you want to share. If you liked this book you may find we have more brilliant ideas for other areas that could help change your life for the better.

You'll find the Infinite Ideas crew waiting for you online at www.infideas.com.

Or if you prefer to write, then send your letters to:
Adventure sports
The Infinite Ideas Company Ltd
36 St Giles, Oxford OX1 3LD, United Kingdom

We want to know what you think, because we're all working on making our lives better too. Give us your feedback and you could win a copy of another *52 Brilliant Ideas* book of your choice. Or maybe get a crack at writing your own.

Good luck. Be brilliant.

Offer one

CASH IN YOUR IDEAS

We hope you enjoy this book. We hope it inspires, amuses, educates and entertains you. But we don't assume that you're a novice, or that this is the first book that you've bought on the subject. You've got ideas of your own. Maybe our author has missed an idea that you use successfully. If so, why not send it to yourauthormissedatrick@infideas.com, and if we like it we'll post it on our bulletin board. Better still, if your idea makes it into print we'll send you four books of your choice or the cash equivalent. You'll be fully credited so that everyone knows you've had another Brilliant Idea.

Offer two

HOW COULD YOU REFUSE?

Amazing discounts on bulk quantities of Infinite Ideas books are available to corporations, professional associations and other organisations.

For details call us on:
+44 (0)1865 514888
fax: +44 (0)1865 514777
or e-mail: info@infideas.com

Where it's at...

UKSKYDIVING

Win a FREE tandem skydive!

See next page for competition to win a FREE Tandem Skydive! Discounts on ALL UK Skydiving Bookings!

UK Skydiving has teamed up with Infinite Ideas to encourage more people to take a giant leap, out of a big plane, from a great height! Since you're reading this book we're presuming that's your cup of tea!

UK Skydiving is the UK's premier freefall and parachute specialist. The company is run by British Parachute Association (BPA) Instructors and offers a range of skydiving courses tailored to suit the individual's skill level and ambition. All jumps take place at BPA affiliated drop zones.

Buying this book has made you eligible for **£20 off** any UK Skydiving booking between now and the end of December 2007, when quoting 'Infinite 52'. Whether you've experienced the skydiving rush before and want to give it another go, or are taking the jump for the first time, with the help of *Adventure sports* and the experts at UK Skydiving, you can make sure that this experience is unforgettable, safe, and what's more, great value.

If you have any questions about the UK Skydiving services or want to book using your special *Adventure sports* discount, please call freephone **0800 1116880** and don't forget to quote the promotional code **'Infinite 52'**. Professional skydivers will be on hand to answer your questions and give you all the advice you need 8am–8pm, seven days a week.

Here are just some of the experiences you can enjoy with your *Adventure sports* discount.

Tandem
Arguably the best way to experience your first freefall! Following a 30-minute ground briefing on the equipment, exiting the aircraft, freefall and landing you are securely attached to an experienced tandem instructor with a 4-point harness system, and board the aircraft. The aircraft will normally climb to between 10,000 and 12,000 feet where you exit and begin to freefall, reaching speeds of up to 120mph as you descend.

AFF – The Accelerated Freefall

This course is a progressive fast track skydiver training programme, which takes you from complete beginner to Category 8 qualified skydiver in 8 jumps.

RAPS – (Ram-Air Progression System)

This is a two day static line parachute course.

For more information on any of the UK Skydiving services please visit their website: **www.ukskydiving.co.uk** To book any of these events please call freephone 0800 1116880 and quote 'Infinite 52'. Please note that this offer excludes wind tunnel experiences. Normal terms and conditions apply.

ADVENTURE SPORTS SKYDIVE COMPETITION

You have the chance to win a FREE TANDEM SKYDIVE, courtesy of UK Skydiving. Just answer the following question:

What does AFF stand for?

A. Adventure Free Fall
B. Accelerated Fast Fall
C. Accelerated Free Fall

Please send your answer to 'Infinite Skydive Competition' 36 St Giles, Oxford, OX1 3LD, United Kingdom or by email to '*freeskydive@infideas.com*', stating your name, address and a contact telephone number.

For more information please visit our website: **www.52brilliantideas.com**

Please note that only one entry is permitted per person. The closing date for entries is 30 November 2006. The winner will be picked at random and notified via telephone. This prize can be claimed within 1 year of the closing date. Terms and conditions apply, please see website for details.

Good Luck!